J.P. Das

J.P. Das

A Creative Journey

By
GANESWAR MISHRA

Translated by
BIKRAM K. DAS

NIYOGI
BOOKS

Published by
NIYOGI BOOKS
D-78, Okhla Industrial Area, Phase-I
New Delhi-110 020, INDIA
Tel: 91-11-26816301, 49327000
Fax: 91-11-26810483, 26813830
email: niyogibooks@gmail.com
website: www.niyogibooksindia.com

Editor: P.K. Jayanthan
Design: Shashi Bhushan Prasad

ISBN: 978-93-85285-10-3
Publication: 2015

Printed at: Niyogi Offset Pvt. Ltd., New Delhi, India

To the many friends and admirers of

J.P. Das

Sketch by Paris Street Artist, 1970

Contents

The Village of No Return

One morning in October 2003, Jagannath Prasad (JP) Das and I set out on a journey to Banpur. He had come to Bhubaneswar from Delhi only the day before, specifically to go to Banpur on an invitation from Nehru Seva Sangh, which was observing the death anniversary of its founder Harihar Ram. He wanted me to accompany him and I did not wish to lose the opportunity to spend some time in his company.

In 2003

FACING PAGE: *Sketch by Sarat Pujari, 1957*

JP has been living in Delhi since he resigned from the Indian Administrative Service in 1984 and comes to Bhubaneswar only when absolutely necessary. I could not understand at first why such a busy person should have accepted the invitation of Nehru Seva Sangh.

He was 67 then. He had his dignified and serene face; free, for the time being, from any health problem; but doctors had advised him against long journeys by car. He could have taken a train to Banpur, but what guarantee was there that he would arrive in time? As punctuality is one of the traits of his character, we took a car. The road was dusty, with frequent breaks where repair works were in progress. But JP seemed to enjoy the trip.

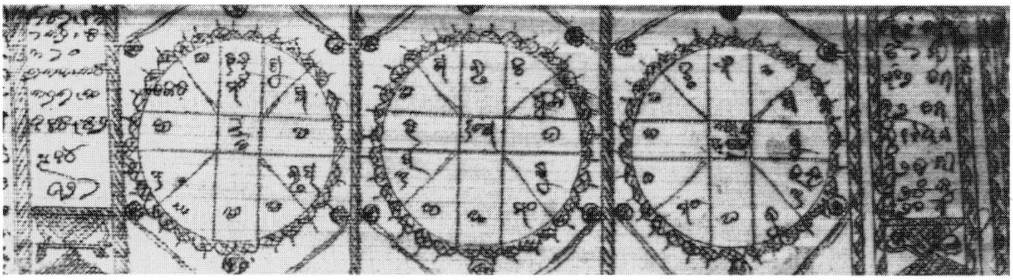

JP's horoscope

There was reason for his enjoyment. It was at Banpur that he was born in 1936. He has carefully preserved his horoscope. He had his primary education in the same town. It was a 'city of memories' for him; though it was not a city, but only a large village when he was a child.

JP's father, Shridhar Das, has written in his autobiography about JP's birth thus,

> The son who had been born during my stay at Boudh died prematurely of diphtheria. Another son was born in 1936 while I was at Banpur. We named him Jagannath Prasad, the gift from Lord Jagannath. It could be said that his education began at the age of four; not formally, but there was much that he had learnt by then. His intelligence and memory were above average. An old-fashioned tutor had been appointed to teach him at home. At the age of 7 he was admitted to the fourth grade and easily obtained high rank in the class. In the meantime, I had lived and worked in many places and finally moved to Cuttack. When he was in the tenth grade I brought him to Cuttack and had him admitted to the Mission School.

Shridhar Das was a teacher in Banpur High School from 1935 to 1942. After several years of teaching in schools, he was appointed Lecturer, and later Professor, in Odia in Christ College, Cuttack, and remained in that position for nearly 20 years. He gained reputation as a lecturer but was better known as a writer. He

JP's father and mother

wrote more than 120 books–criticism, dictionaries, grammar, textbooks, translation, biographies, and an autobiography–which are testimony to his dedication and commitment to Odia language. This enormous output would not have been possible if he had not lived a disciplined life.

The influence of JP's father on him is evident. JP has written in this connection, 'Our home was full of books and old magazines. In addition, many writers visited us and there was always a literary environment at home. This may have drawn me to literature.'

JP's father, who was equally disciplined, undoubtedly provided the inspiration for his life. This is what made his amazing literary creativity possible. But he was different from his father in many other ways. Although his father believed that his birth was due to Jagannath's blessings, JP never showed devotion to any temple or religious institution. However, his respect for his father was undiminished. His siblings and he collaborated in setting up the Shridhar Das Memorial Library in the premises of the Utkal Sahitya Samaj (Utkal literary association) in Cuttack. He was also instrumental in the institution of Shridhar Das Memorial Lectures at the Utkal University in 1995.

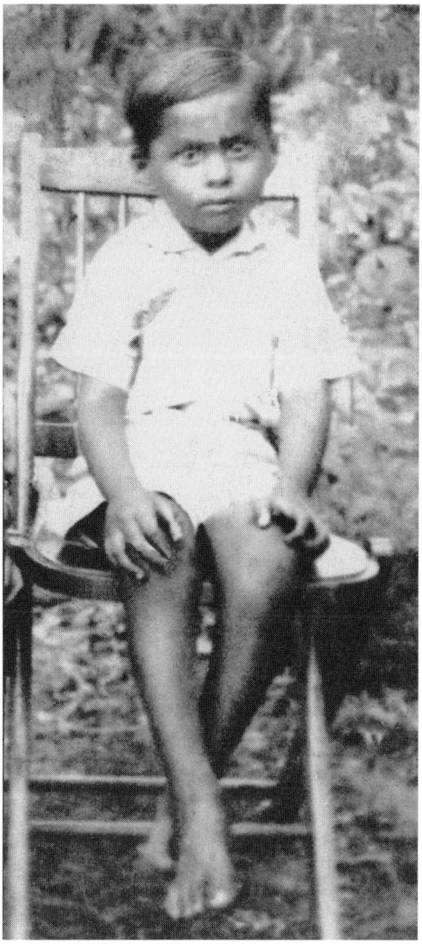

In 1940

Nehru Seva Sangh, Banpur, was established in 1947 by Harihar Ram, his elder brother Baidyanath Ram, and JP, with Pandit Godavarish Mishra as its President. The children of the village took leading role in a variety of social activities, from cleaning the village to creating public awareness against superstitions. JP was only about 10 years old then. The Nehru Seva Sangh is a vast organization through which hundreds of destitute, orphaned, and physically handicapped children belonging to the oppressed castes and aboriginal tribes have been benefited. Its efforts at providing shelter and education to the poor and turning them into productive citizens have been praiseworthy. The organisation celebrated its Golden Jubilee in 1997.

Harihar Ram had been JP's classmate and childhood friend. Unfortunately, he passed away in 2002. I did not know until we reached Banpur that a marble bust of Harihar Ram had been put up in the Sangh's premises on the occasion of his first death anniversary and JP was to unveil the statue. I got the impression, however, that he had not been informed of it either.

It was mainly Harihar through his organisation that helped to consolidate JP's links with Banpur. Letters had regularly been exchanged between the two. JP was the patron of Nehru Seva Sangh, providing financial and other assistance as and when possible. But he had never mentioned this to anyone. I received some inkling of this connection from letters written by Harihar. Here are some excerpts from some of these letters,

With father, sister, and younger brother, in 1942

Dear Jagannath Babu,

Please accept my greetings. I have written two letters to you in the meantime but am worried as there is no reply. You must have been extremely busy. The Annual Meeting of the Nehru Seva Sangh will be held at Banpur on the 10th of next month (10.9.83). I am enclosing the formal letter of invitation, but I extend my personal invitation to you as well, which I hope you will surely accept. I write this letter at the request of all the members of the Sangh.

I have a special request to convey. All of us want you not only to preside over this year's meeting but also to accept permanent Presidentship of the Sangh. In view of what the Sangh has been able to achieve, I am sure you will agree that it deserves to have you as its President. As a friend and companion, and as a worker of the Sangh, I hope you will not turn down this request. I look forward to an early reply from you, and I hope it will not be negative.

15.11.2000
I will never forget your kind visit to the Sangh with Sri Balbir Mathur. I have become so emotional about it that I do not find words to describe it. It is like recovering old forgotten memories, like a pauper receiving a bonanza. When you come to Orissa next, please let me know so that we could meet. At this fag end of my lonely life, only friends like you are my only support in my remaining days.

29.7.2001
I spoke to Sri Balbir Mathur and briefed him about the coconut plantation work here. I also told him about the terrible floods. I have faxed him a list of our requirements, a copy of which I am enclosing. Please talk to him. I again express my gratitude that through your efforts Nehru Seva Sangh, which you had started, is getting full support for its projects.

Affectionately,
Harihar

With Balbir Mathur after super cyclone, in 2000

That day, JP formally unveiled the statue of the late Harihar Ram. Addressing the assembled children and other guests he said,

> Today, for the first time, I have come to Banpur and found Harihar missing. Our friendship goes back to more than 60 years and he has always been someone I respected deeply. While the rest of us were engrossed in worldly affairs, it was Harihar alone who kept alive the dreams of our childhood by dedicating himself to the service of the people. Whenever we met, after long intervals, he gave me news of the Seva Sangh's activities and we discussed what more could be done to further its goals. I have been doing whatever I can at Delhi to aid its activities.

Some of JP's former classmates at Banpur High School are no more and he has lost touch with some of the others. Sixty years have passed since he left Banpur and it is only natural for old links to have been weakened.

Muralidhar Satpathy, a former Chief Engineer, is one of JP's close friends from those days. He is deeply interested in art and

Garlanding Harihar Ram's bust

literature. Post-retirement he lives in Bhubaneswar. Remembering his childhood in Banpur he says,

> Jagannath Prasad Das, whom I have always called Jagana, is a childhood friend. We have known each other since 1943. My father, Laxmidhar Satpathy, and Jagana's father, Shridhar Das, were both teachers at Banpur High School. We lived in neighbouring houses and studied in the same class. Our practice was to study together, play together, and roam together. Jagana's brilliance was evident even in those early days.

JP has not written his autobiography yet. Banpur is not mirrored in his poems, short stories, novels, or plays, as it has in some of the poems of Godavarish Mishra or Krishnachandra Tripathy. But surely, glimpses of Banpur can be found in JP's poem 'Pila Dina' (childhood days). Here is the poem,

In 1948

Childhood Days

Houses stood in rows, hands clasped together
As the mysterious sunlight
Played hide-and-seek with the clouds
The whirlwind got stuck in the branches
Of the tamarind tree and the raven flew away
Clutching emptiness in its beak

The chanting of multiplication tables was drowned
In the 'tupur-tupur' of raindrops
White cranes shook their wings and flew out of nests
At the last trill
Of the wandering gypsy's song
And out of the pages of the alphabet book
Wild buffaloes came swarming

Tiny round letters bloomed like janhi flowers
On children's slates
Lilies from the garden of nursery rhymes
Sprouted through the covers of school bags
Paper boats folded by fond maternal uncles
Sank unseen in the maelstrom of dreams
While the squirrel nibbled away at the kite's dangling thread

The palm tree extended long hands
To touch the first star
From the grass-hopper's leg
Dropped a thousand winking glow worms
Brother Fox's shrill trumpeting was drowned
In the harsh croaking of Auntie Frog
The stubborn child howled and howled
Demanding that the moon be tethered in the cow shed

But the Uncle in the sky refused to be trapped
It wouldn't drop into Kanhu's palms
The rabbit in the moon scampered away
To run a race with the tortoise

Childhood retreated with tearful eyes
Into the thickest forest
The lotus kept slithering away
Into the depths of the fairy-pond
Childhood sank without a trace
Losing its way among the wild berry's thorns
Lost among dusty whirlwinds
Lost in the gleam of the witch's eye
Carried away on butterfly's wings

Childhood went, innocent and untarnished
Riding the cart, along the road
To the unknown kingdom's
Village of No Return

The heart of the poem, of course, is the 'Village of No Return' – the village to which JP has not returned and never will. Which other village can it be but Banpur? His father's original village was Naeeguan (village by the river), near Kakatpur, Puri. But JP never had anything to do with it.

On this morning in October 2003, JP was returning to Banpur. Though lives in the metropolis of Delhi, JP returns frequently to his village, his town, to Odisha – in his dreams and imagination, if not literally. He writes in Odia. He has always been intertwined with the literature, culture, and life of Odisha. He searches for his creative identity between the expanse and impersonality of the metropolis and the intimacy of rural Odisha. He does not inhabit that village – but surely it is not, for him, the village of no return.

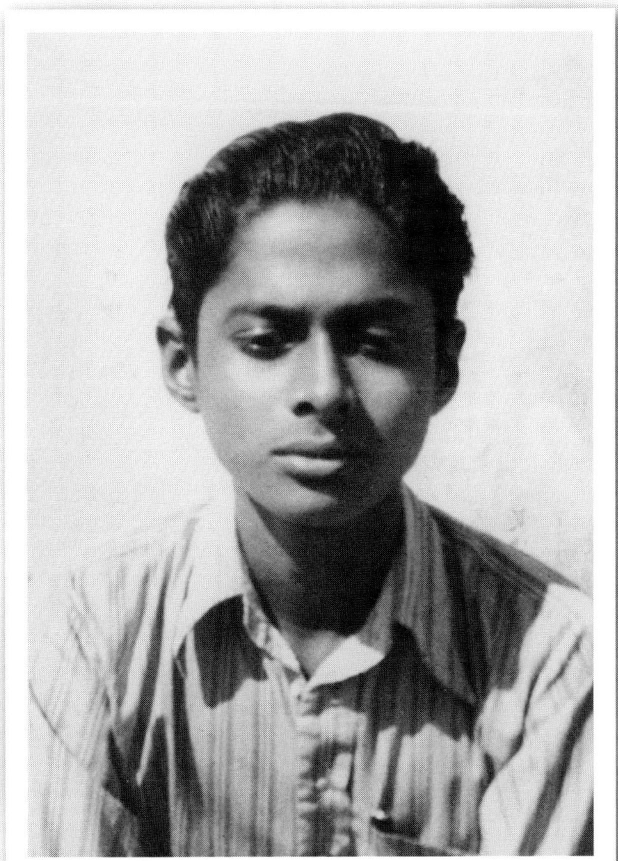

In 1950

In the Embrace of Two Rivers

In his poem 'Bandira swadesha chinta' (the prisoner remembers his homeland), Gopabandhu Das describes the city of Cuttack as 'Mahanadi-neera-neela-basana' (clothed in the Mahanadi's blue robes), which is to imply that it is the Mahanadi that gives Cuttack its identity. JP has a poem on Cuttack too, in which he describes the city somewhat differently. In his poem, Cuttack is said to 'lie embraced by two rivers' – the Mahanadi and the Kathajodi.

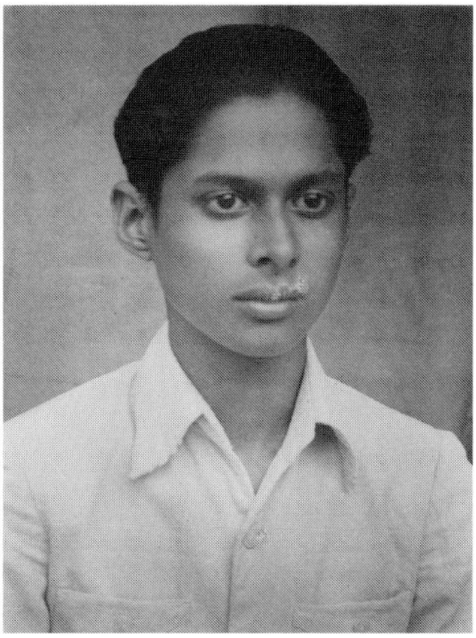

In 1951

FACING PAGE: *Sketch by Serbjeet Singh*

JP lived in Cuttack from 1948 to 1955. He moved to Cuttack after his father Shridhar Das left Banpur and this was where JP spent the rest of his school days and a part of his life as a college student. In the words of Shridhar Das,

> After having wandered through many places I finally reached Cuttack. When Jagannath was in the tenth class I had him admitted to Mission High School in Cuttack, and later to Christ College. It was as a student of this school that he appeared at the Matriculation examination and obtained the second rank in the university. I was teaching at Christ College then and got him admitted to

> the same college in order to save on expenses. He could not do as well in the I.A. examination. I seem to recall that he obtained the fifth rank. Thereafter, I was obliged to bring him to Ravenshaw College, because our college offered Honours courses only in Odia and English. He took up Honours in Economics and passed the B.A. examination with Second Class Honours.

The father describes the son as being a good student during his school and college days. Every father wants his son to do well in studies and then to have a successful professional life. This is what Shridhar Das wanted for his son, too. He has written almost nothing about the poetry and the paintings that JP produced while he was a student. Those who knew JP intimately during those days in Cuttack recall that he was an outstanding student, with a talent for poetry and painting, although rather shy. I have known him for almost 30 years. We have been intimate, though we are not of the same age, but he has never spoken to me of his achievements as a student.

My friend and classmate Lakshmidhar Mishra has some wonderful reminiscences of JP's student days. Lakshmidhar was a brilliant student himself. Like JP he joined the Indian Administrative Service and retired as Secretary in the Ministry of Labour, Government of India. He lives in Delhi now. This is what he remembers of JP's student days in Christ College,

> My elder brother Dr Shrinibas Mishra was a Lecturer in Odia at Christ College during 1951–1954 and Jagannath Babu was his student. As I was then studying in a village school I never had the opportunity of meeting him, but I had heard a great deal about him – about his imaginativeness, his open attitudes, his aesthetic sense, and academic brilliance. At a very young age, therefore, I had made him my ideal. Later, my brother was posted to Fakirmohan College, Balasore, and while staying with him I saw, hanging on a wall in his bedroom, the

Farewell Address presented to him when he left Christ College. I was told that it had been composed by his favourite student, Jagannath Prasad Das. Between 1955 and 1958 I read this address several times and each time I felt overwhelmed by the deep respect that a student had shown for his teacher. The address was beautifully written by hand, in perfect straight lines, and short sentences. This expression of a fresh, transparent mind had the impact of a painting on me.

In my life I have come across many surprising and unexpected events. Years later, quite unexpectedly, I happened to see an answer paper that Jagannath Babu had written for his I.A. examination. I have never seen another paper that was so well written. The handwriting was a work of art. The sentences were simple, with not a word wasted. The treatment of the subject and the style were attractive. He had been awarded 70 per cent marks for this paper, which was unheard of for a paper in literature in those days. His teacher had preserved it carefully, as a model for the next generation of students. Jagannath Babu became my ideal for all time to come.

With college friends. JP in front row, first from left

One of JP's teachers at Christ College was the well-known critic, Pathani Pattanayak. In his autobiography *Jibanara Chala Patha* (the pathways of life) he has reminisced, like a true teacher, about JP as 'a first class student'. A contemporary of JP, the retired professor of philosophy, Ganeswar Das, becomes somewhat emotional when writing about the student life of his friend. He says, 'When I was a student of I.A., our neighbour was Pandit Shridhar Das, Professor of Odia. His eldest son, Jagannath and I were close friends, although he was three years younger. Jagannath was extraordinarily brilliant.'

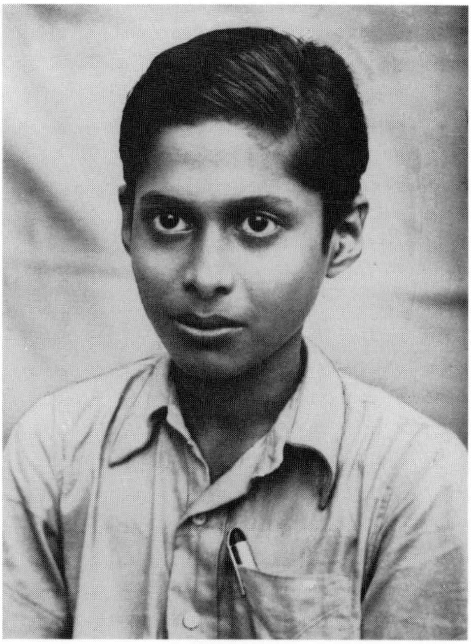

In 1950

Today JP is known for his poetry, short stories, novels, and plays, but the dedication and scholarship displayed in his research have remained undiminished. This is most evident in his art criticism. By combining critical and creative writing he has given evidence of his versatility. In 1979 he was awarded the Homi Bhabha Fellowship for conducting research on the patachitra paintings of Puri.

He has always been an extraordinary scholar – not just during his years in Cuttack but throughout his life. Study, research, and inquiry have formed one stream in his life and creativity the other.

He gave ample evidence of his poetic talent even as a college student. He wrote more than a hundred poems between 1948 and 1955, of which about half remain unpublished to this day. Some of them are still available with the poet in manuscript form. In 1951, *Stabaka* (hymns/bouquet), a slender volume containing 49 poems, was published. Here are some lines from a poem in this collection.

Creativity Awakens

This new symphony of light has awakened
The thrill of creativity
Within the sightless interior of my being
The straying traveller has found his path
And discovered the beautiful earth beneath the obscuring veil
The glory of creation dances before my eyes
Oh, how I wish I could fly like a bird!
I have found the path
And the great mission of creation has begun!

In 1954

The printing and cover of *Stabaka* were tastefully done. But those who are acquainted with JP's poetry written during the next six decades may find this volume no different from the work of any other poet. The poems are written in the traditional rhyming verse that was popular at the time. The subject matter is chiefly nature, love, history, etc.

JP published some stories and essays along with his poems but it was mainly in poetry that he found his identity. He gives to *Pratham Purush* (first person), published in 1971, the distinction of being his first published work of poetry. All the poems composed by him earlier, published or unpublished, were put aside as being 'immature' and so none of the poems written during his Cuttack period find a place in *Pratham Purush.*

A poet or writer may not always be the best judge of his own work. Many readers have found a rich vein of emotion in his pre-*Pratham Purush* poetry. His contemporary, Purna Chandra Hota, former Chairman of the Union Public Service Commission, says,

> I remember the poem 'Chilika', published in the Christ College Magazine in 1952. After I had read this poem a number of times I was convinced it would find a pre-eminent place in Odia poetry. Many years later, I wrote to many litterateurs in Odisha, as well as to the Principal of Christ College and the Collector of Cuttack, requesting them to send me a photo copy of the poem. They wrote back saying that the magazine was not to be traced anywhere.

Perhaps JP does not himself believe that many people read those early poems of his. After many years, Professor Maheswar Mohanty, an exponent of children's literature who retired in 2002 after teaching Odia in Christ College for many years. wrote a letter, providing a valuable insight into JP's poetry written during 1948–55 and is worth quoting at length.

> When I was a student in a rural high school, I had not given much thought to what I would become in future. I wrote poems and stories which were published in periodicals and was drawn to literature and eventually teaching literature and writing criticism became my profession. I came to know many writers, brought them to my classes and introduced them to my students. I was, however, never able to find the one poet who had inspired this insignificant being (the writer himself) more than any others. For 50 years I have carried on my silent quest, but in vain. From time to time this elusive name peeps, like the new moon, into my consciousness, only to retreat again. And again, from time to time, a hand comes from behind and grips me by the shoulder; a voice murmurs into my ears a few lines of a poem I had read during my adolescence, but when I turn my head and try to see who it is, it would have disappeared. One such poem was,

Who are you, Stone Beauty,
Reposing in this land of sand-dunes?
Could you be the nymph Urvashi, bearing the curse of youth,
With the tranquil sky above and the bowed earth below?
Bathed in moonlight, oh, Maid of the Evening!

In 1948

This was the first poem in a little book that had no illustration on its cover but only three letters from the Odia alphabet. I do not remember the name of the book; only that of the poet—Jagannath Prasad Das. For half a century I have been silently thinking of the poet, like a character in some novel.

While I was in school, several of my poems appeared in the Young Readers' section of the periodical *Aasantaa Kaali* (tomorrow), then published from Calcutta. I had built up a sizable collection of back-numbers of the periodical. Jagannath Prasad Das's poems were regularly published in *Aasantaa Kaali* during 1953–54. I can still recall faintly a few lines,

Today I hear the call
Of the traveller's nest
Among distant mountains
Whose dream has made my heart restless

I do not remember the title of the poem. But my adolescent fancies were stirred by another poem in that volume, of which also I remember a few lines,

Beneath the blood-stream
Rush legions of nameless microbes,
Robbing the human body
Of flesh and blood.

These lines had appealed to me strongly. My memory has never been good and I had not taken care to get the lines by heart. Still, the words and lines of a poem that has touched the heart may linger on in the adolescent mind. A portion of another poem runs like this,

> *The cannons thunder, the atoms roar*
> *Destruction raises its fiery head*
> *And man has enslaved man*

I cannot remember more. My memory has grown feeble with age. I do not even remember whether this poem was from *Asanta Kaali* or from that book with three letters on the cover. I have been unable to connect the Jagannath Prasad Das of today with the poet 50 years ago....The Jagannath Prasad Das of those years must surely have been a mature person even then. Where did we lose him? No one has any news of him. With such firm delusions in my head, I abandoned him then and there.

About two years ago I asked this question of Prof. Pathani Pattanayak. In a voice tinged with doubt he said, 'A Jagannath Prasad used to write poetry when he was a student. It could be the same person. He writes modern poetry now.' I had found an answer to my queries at last. Had I asked him this question earlier, I would not have had to waste those long years in confused speculation, or in the mists of uncertainty. Jagannath Prasad had written poetry in his childhood; his books had been published when he was in his youth. And then another event ... I had neither his telephone number nor his address, but I managed to get both from someone. And I found my answer. The name of that little book with the three letters on the cover was *Stabaka*. So the renowned modern poet, painter, researcher, and author of *Pratham Purush, Anya Sabu Mrityu, Je Jaahaara Nirjanataa, Desha Kaala Paatra* and other books was none other than the poet who had kept my adolescence in thrall with his *Stabaka*, 50 years ago. The two were one and the same person!

Here are some lines from two other JP poems of the same period.

Let Him Live Today

This child who has taken birth on our fevered earth
Let him live today
He who has arrived unscathed, bearing tidings of the future
Let him live!

Let Us Shake Hands

I have seen you, my friend, on the city streets
Standing at the gates of government offices;
On the tram or train, at home or outside,
On the unceasing journey of today's peripatetic man.

Friend, I see you inside the nameless hotel,
Holding a half cup of tea and today's newspaper,
Inhaling all the pleasure of the morning
With the smoke of cheap cigarettes.

Dragging those two tired feet, in season or out,
Scanning every 'ad' that promises 'Situation Vacant'
Filling up the dust bin in every office
With mountains of applications

During his student days JP's poetry was published in periodicals such as *Dagara, Prajatantra, Dainik Aasha,* and *Kumkum* (the last one being published from Bombay). *Aagaami* was the favourite periodical of left-leaning students. The president of its editorial committee was Manoj Das and JP was a prominent member. Later, Manoj Das became famous as the editor of periodicals such as *Diganta* and *The Heritage* and as the spokesperson of Marxist ideology as well as Sri Aurobindo's philosophy. But JP was not keen to take up any editorial responsibility or become the voice of any 'ism' or ideology.

When JP left Cuttack in 1955 he had established himself as the leading poet of the younger generation. I quote the following comments by Chintamani Behera, journalist, poet, critic, and academic, published in *Aagaami* in January 1955,

> There are many streams in modern poetry; nevertheless, most modern poets have created meaningful poetry in their respective streams. Several of these modern poets are 'experimentalists', some are 'naturalists' and others 'progressives'. Among the many young and skilled poets of today, barring those of the Sabuj (green) movement, are Ananta Patnaik, Binodchandra Nayak, Gyanindra Verma, Kunjabihari Dash, Janaki Mohanty, Benudhar Rout, Manoj Das, Umashankar Panda, Jagannath Prasad Das, Ramakanta Rath, Kumari Tulasi Das, Krushna Charan Behera, and Durga Prasad Parida.'

In the March 1971 issue of *Naba Rabi*, poet Bibekananda Jena had written in his essay 'Pratham Purush: A Personal Viewpoint', 'Very few people know that once upon a time, Jagannath Prasad Das was considered a greater poet than his contemporary Ramakanta Rath.'

About 20 years after he left Cuttack, JP composed the poem 'Cuttack', in memory of the city. Here is the poem in its entirety,

Memories return when I'm here
Many memories
The idle days
Of love poems scribbled in notebooks
The pocketful of spring breezes
Moments of empty reverie, gazing at the sky
Days when one dedicated

Fistfuls of mellow sunshine to others
Known faces come back to mind
Faces seen long ago
Those whose feet were hobbled
By the enchantment of gazing
At the rainbow overhead
Sitting on a bench by the river's edge
Those who were left behind
Among the crowds at the Bali Jatra
Those who were lost
While flying coloured handkerchiefs in the sky
Or those who were trapped
By sorrowful moments
While coming out of cinema halls
With eyes full of tears

When one tries to move forward today
One is tied down to the place
By the sari's aanchal
Fluttering through the rickshaw
The multi-coloured sensations
You have left behind bar your way
Like the gates of the level-crossing
Consciousness is slowed
Amid the crush of traffic
The eyes are forced to linger
On the changing landscape of the roadside
And the mind quietly accepts
The compulsions of growing up

Everything looks familiar
Sunlight creeping up the embankments
On tip-toe
The beggar sitting by the road-side
Looking at the rags of flying clouds in the sky

The kite, with its string cut
Descending slowly onto the battered roof
The deity's oblation
Trickling through temple floors
Mingle with the city's sewage

Justice is bought and sold
Amid portable tea-stalls
Offerings to Chandi, the city's patron goddess
Are washed away in the rain
The learned discourse
In the coffee house at College Square
Comes to an abrupt halt
The terror of the Deluge
Quivering at the overflowing Kathjodi's banks
Drowns the newspaper-vendor's call

Coming out of the hospital
Feet come to a halt at the crossroads
Where all paths lead to oblivion
No one looks back
Taking the Mahanadi water in hollowed palms
You offer it to ancestors

At some unknown hour
Summer goes out and mingles
With the uneasy intimacy of unseasonal rain
Lamp-posts grow older
Forgotten memories play hide-and-seek
Among the mazes of unknown lanes

Within the embrace of two rivers
The city rests, unconcerned
The world remains ever the same
While history is transformed

At Trafalgar Square, 1970

The Range of Relationships

In 1952, while still a student of Christ College, JP set out with some friends on a trip to Dhabaleswar, the island in the Mahanadi on which stands a temple dedicated to Shiva, the White God, after whom the place is named. Each year, a fair is held here to celebrate the Bada Osha festival. Dhabaleswar is a famous place of pilgrimage.

Although JP carries no religious baggage, Dhabaleswar was to him a literary pilgrimage, for this was where Shashibhusan Ray, the leading Odia essayist and the son of the great poet Radhanath Ray,

At Dhabaleswar, in 1952. JP standing third from right

FACING PAGE: *Sketch by Prabhakar Machwe*

was living in solitude, serving his literary muse. He was 89 then and had practically lost his eye-sight. JP had hoped to spend some time with Shashibhusan Babu and to collect his autograph – perhaps to be photographed with him.

After his visit to Dhabaleswar, JP wrote the following poem, written while Shashibhusan Babu was alive, which was published in *Prajatantra* on 6 September 1953. Sadly, Shashibhushan had passed away two days earlier.

Shashibhusan

No sound here of human voices
Life has forgotten
The teeming world outside
Alone on this island
Lost in silent contemplation
Of the motherland
Dwells a solitary devotee
A wild jasmine
Hidden from the eye
Filling the air with its fragrance.

Here, in secrecy, behind the clouds,
The 'shashi' of the literary sky smiles,
Ignored by civilization,
His gifts to society forgotten
Banished by his own people,
Waiting for death on this lonely island.

Shortly after JP's return to Cuttack, Shashibhushan Babu wrote a letter to JP's father, Shridhar Das, recounting affectionately, in a wavering hand, his meeting with the young visitors from Christ College.

Before JP's poem was published, Kunjabihari Dash, the well-known Odia poet, had already written a poem on Shashi Babu, which was published in the periodical *Sahakaar*. I came across the poem in the Ramakrishna Mission library at Puri while I was a student at Puri. I still recall some of its lines,

> *The light is gone from one eye*
> *While the other is about to set*
> *But the pen remains active*
> *Praise be to you, Shashibhusan Ray!*
>
> *Hirakud may yield golden fruit*
> *And Duduma with gold may be covered*
> *But never again shall Odisha find*
> *Another Shashibhushan Ray*

Kunjabihari Dash was nearly 40 years when he wrote this poem while JP was only 17 when his poem was written. But his eagerness, even at this tender age, to mingle with writers and poets is testimony to his own creative inclinations. He has always attached the highest importance to organising literary activities and developing personal relationships with poets, writers, and artists. His circle of contacts among creative personages, both established and emerging, in Odisha as well as the rest of the country and abroad, has been extensive. He either had or still has close contacts with film director Satyajit Ray, novelist Mulk Raj Anand, poet and lyricist Gulzaar, art critics Kapila Vatsyayan, Joanna Williams, Eberhard Fischer, theatre director Ram Gopal Bajaj, poet Brajanath Rath, actor Sarat Pujari, and painter and writer Dinanath Pathy. His friends include politicians, administrators, academics, and social activists. He is well-known for his affability even towards those whom he knows only slightly.

For some years now I have seen that each time JP comes to Bhubaneswar from Delhi, there are crowds of admirers waiting to meet him. He knows the art of maintaining relationships with established as well as budding writers. But I have repeatedly heard the accusation, 'JP spends so little time in Bhubaneswar!' Many people are, therefore, unable to meet him on these visits.

Evidence of JP's affectionate dealing with friends comes from two of his associates. In the words of Sudhir Kumar Bijayendra Narayan, alias 'Japani', an engineer and writer of fiction,

> 'Go to the hostel of any college, you will find the best students constantly carrying thick books, trying desperately to memorise their contents. You will be told that they are preparing for the IAS examination. This is reputedly the most prized of all government services. Once you are in, all kinds of opportunities come to you unasked; and so the highest aspiration for any student is to secure a job which has the suffix IAS, IPS, or Allied Services attached to it.
>
> I began my career in government service in 1962–63. Years later, I heard that a senior IAS officer had resigned from the service to become a full-time writer and painter. As he had earlier been Secretary to the Government in our own department, this event was discussed vigorously among my colleagues.
>
> 'Who is this incredible person?' I asked and was informed that his name was J.P. Das.
>
> It was only natural for me to be curious about someone who was so deeply dedicated to literature and art. A feeling of devotion, mixed with affection, was growing within me. I first saw him at a meeting at Bhubaneswar (he has little faith in meetings or committees). His slim frame, clothed in jeans and tee-shirt, seemed that of a college student; I could not believe that this was indeed J.P. Das. For the next two days, I followed him like a shadow to every meeting and club that he went to, charmed by his behaviour and speech.
>
> Every visit of JP to Bhubaneswar is regulated to the nearest minute. From the moment he touches down at the airport to the time of his departure, every engagement

Abhyudaya Patha Chakra, 1951. JP, standing, second from right

> is gone through precisely on time. A specific time is assigned to each meeting and appointment, discussion, lunch and dinner engagement, cultural programme, and chat session with friends – nothing is overlooked. This has helped me to understand how this amazing person found the mental strength and courage to sacrifice the power and glory of the IAS and step into the world of literature and art. For one who has measured out his life in hours and minutes and devoted every moment to creative activity, the highest seat of power is insignificant.

Acharya Bhabananda, writer, thinker, and social worker, sees JP somewhat differently,

> I do not know Jagannath Prasad Das intimately; we may have met only two or three times. We have exchanged a few letters, but how much can a letter tell you about

> the depths of an artist? Jagannath Babu's pen and paint-brush have transcended the limitations of time. It cannot have been easy for him to overcome the attraction of emotions and it may be this resilience that distinguishes him from others. It is not easy for a reader like me to appreciate his delicate artistic touch. I have always respected him for his artistic personality. In my opinion, he is a deep creative artist, often reaching the realms of philosophy.

At Christ College, JP was involved in the activities of the Abhyudaya Patha Chakra (Abhyudaya study circle). Several literary seminars were organised through this Patha Chakra and many valuable books published. In the words of its founder, Pathani Pattanayak,

> When I found several of the students of the first year class profoundly interested in literature, I gathered them together and formed a literary association, which was named Abhyudaya Patha Chakra. The earliest among them were Jagannath Prasad Das, Sudhanshu Routray, Bibekananda Das, and some others. We used to assemble on every holiday at the samshan (funeral ground) at Sati Chowra. My friends, Professors Shrinibas Mishra, Shridhar Das, and Banambar Acharya, used to participate in the discussion to enthuse the students. Jagannath stood out easily among them. He was extremely talented and distinguished himself at the matriculation examination. Inspired by his father, Prof. Shridhar Das, he had started writing poetry at an early age and astonishingly, had already published a collection of poems. His dedication to poetry and academics ran concurrently. In those days, students were given assignments to work on at every tutorial, and these assignments were examined by tutors during the next session. Jagannath invariably turned in the best piece

of writing. His oral presentations, delivered at sessions of the Patha Chakra in the presence of his professors, were outstanding. His line of thinking, while analysing and critiquing literary creations, was always original. Most students were reluctant to participate in these discussions but Jagannath was never afraid to present his own opinion.

In a letter written to JP in May 1993, writer Manoj Das refers to such a literary discussion held in 1952, 'Although we seldom meet, I have the highest regard for you. The reason may lie in a literary discussion organized by you during the fifties. You were a young student then. I was living in either Balasore or Puri but happened to be in Cuttack when one of your programmes was on. That was when we first met, near Jobra.'

Poetry workshop, Bhubaneswar, 1994

In 1984, JP and several of his friends in Delhi formed The Poetry Society (India), of which JP was the guiding spirit. Its secretary was H.K. Kaul and Keshav Mallik its first president. JP became the president during 1986 and 2000, after which he continues to be a member of the managing committee as well as an advisor.

The Poetry Society (India) has been organising poetry competitions at the national level since 1988 in collaboration with the British Council. One of the aims of the Society is to guide and encourage young poets to write poetry. It also publishes *The Journal of the Poetry Society (India)* in English.

In 1992, JP conceived the idea of organizing workshops for budding poets and was successful in obtaining the necessary financial support from the Ministry of Human Resources. Since then poetry workshops have been convened regularly through his efforts. A workshop is held each year in Bhubaneswar, Odisha where young poets from different parts of Odisha are invited to participate.

Pre-eminent among the poets emerging from these workshops is Pritidhara Samal, who was awarded the Yuba Pratibha (young talent) prize by the Sahiya Akademi, Odisha. The Akademi has published her collection of poems, *Khela* (play). This is how she describes her experiences at a Poetry Workshop,

> This happened 13 years ago. I was very young then but had dreams of becoming a poet. The love of poetry filled my mind and soul. A three-day poetry workshop, organized by the Poetry Society (India), was held in December 1994 at the Regional Institute of Education, Bhubaneswar.

With Pritidhara Samal in Poetry Workshop, 2007

Many young girls and boys from all over Odisha had come to participate. One of these young poets, who has succeeded in creating an independent space for herself in the field of Odia literature is Ipsita Sarangi. This three-day workshop brought out many hidden talents into the open. Nearly all the reputed poets and writers of Odisha were there to provide guidance to participants. Behind the entire organization of the programme and the vast assembly of writers was the guiding hand of Dr Das.

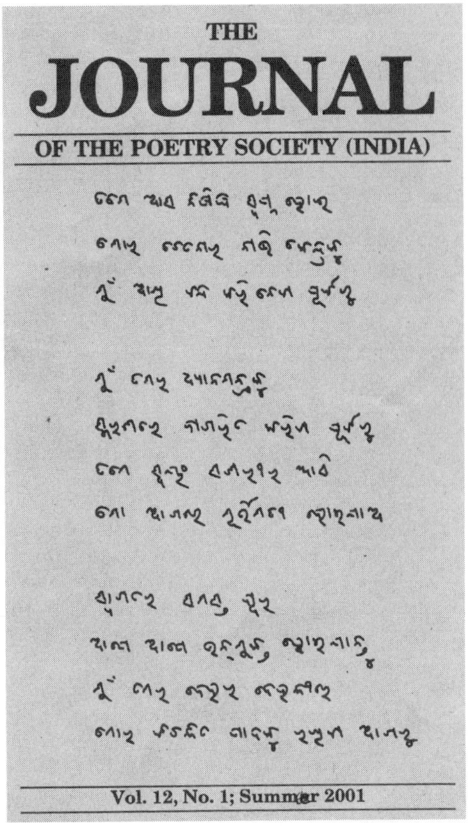

The Journal of the Poetry Society (India), Summer 2001 issue

One of the words in my poem was *keeta-drashta* (moth-eaten). The flow of criticism came to a halt on that word. What would have been the appropriate word to use? This became the subject of debate among the poets on the dais. Finally, Dr Das asked for a dictionary to be fetched. His fatherly affection, his expert advice and guidance, charmed everyone. He went from room to room, inquiring whether we were comfortable, whether we had eaten, etc. Even during the evenings, he would come to find out if the arrangements were satisfactory.

The most attractive feature of his personality were his eyes. His glance was so sharp that it seemed to penetrate the heart. There was a wonderful shine in those eyes. It was not impossible for one to become charmed if one kept on looking at those eyes.

Allahabad: From Study and Teaching to the IAS

In 1955 JP obtained the B.A. Honours degree in Economics as a student of Ravenshaw College, Cuttack. In those days, i.e. nearly 60 years ago, the number of M.A. degree holders was not large in Odisha. With the exception of Ravenshaw College and Utkal University, few institutions offered M.A. degrees. Even here courses were offered in only a few subjects. As no one had heard of television, computers, or Internet, one could not even dream of taking up Information Technology, Electronics, Management, or Media as career options. For a good student, the only choices were teaching, the civil services, medicine, or engineering. There was no one in Odisha to advise students on their career plans.

At Allahabad, 1956

FACING PAGE: *Sketch by Asim Basu*

JP's father, Shridhar Das, seems to have had a hand in guiding his son's career until his B.A. days. In his words,

> The problem now was to decide where he should go for his postgraduate studies, and in which subject. He

> was determined to study Political Science at Allahabad University but I was reluctant to let him go. How could an 18-year old, in rather frail health, manage so far away from home? But he secured a scholarship of Rs 40 a month and travelled to Allahabad with some other Odia students.

Jagannath Prasad was admitted to the Department of Political Science at Allahabad University. He was already known as an outstanding student and a leading young poet when he left Odisha. How did he feel in a totally different environment, so far away from Cuttack, the life-centre of Odia literature and culture? We learn something of this from the accounts of his contemporaries at Allahabad.

Purna Chandra Hota reminisces,

> Jagannath Babu joined the Department of Political Science at Allahabad University in 1955 and obtained the M.A. degree in 1957, obtaining the first rank in the first class. Even after that, he was a boarder in the Sir Ganganath Jha Hostel. His intention was to prepare for the IAS examination.

A classmate of JP's was Balram Chandra Rastogi, who later entered the Indian Revenue Service and retired as Chairman of the Board of Customs and Excise. He says,

> J.P. Das was admitted to the M.A. course in Political Science in 1955. He was shy and reserved, with a child's face. Studies were his first priority, but in his limited circle of friends he was extremely popular. His contacts with friends of those years long past have remained unbroken. Even his close friends may not have been fully aware of the poet's sensibility that lay within him. They

At Sir Ganganath Jha Hostel, Allahabad, 1955. Second from right, Sarat Pujari; fourth from left, JP

might have known him as an agnostic, who tended to be argumentative. His sympathy for the downtrodden was well known. There were a few sensational events taking place at the university in those days and life passed smoothly in chatting over breakfast at the coffee house.

He obtained the highest position at the M.A. examination in 1957 and became a lecturer in the Department of Political Science. But his career in teaching was short-lived, as he got into the IAS in 1958. Thereafter, he bade farewell to the world of administration and was lost in the world of literature and art.

But it is Sarat Pujari who has provided the most intimate glimpses of JP's life at Allahabad. Sarat Pujari is a legend in the world of Odia cinema, who has not yet received, either from the government or society, the honour due to him. But he has always remained indifferent to public adulation.

This is how Sarat Pujari writes about JP's life (and his own) at Allahabad,

During the decade from 1950 to 1960, most Odia students went to Patna, Calcutta, Benares, Lucknow, or Allahabad for higher studies. Nearly 50 of them came to Allahabad each year. Being the second oldest, Allahabad University was well known all over the country. Its students, who generally secured high ranks in the Civil Services examinations, were held in esteem. They distinguished themselves not only in the academic disciplines but also in non-traditional degree or diploma courses in art, music, etc. Students from Odisha, who invariably performed well in studies as well as the Civil Services examinations, were greatly liked by their professors.

When I came to the university in 1954, the Odia Chhatra Samaj (Odia students' association) had among its senior members Dr Tribikram Pati (Mathematics), Naba Kumar Mishra (Law), Chandrashekar Mishra (Economics), and Ramakanta Mishra (Political Science). They helped to make ourselves feel at home in the university and the hostels. This tradition has continued since 1945.

Since my childhood I have been fond of acting and painting, and these hobbies helped to make me popular among students after the displays on 'induction' night. Within two months, I had joined the diploma course in painting in addition to the M.A. (Economics) course. JP often came to my room in the hostel and we talked about acting and painting. Although he had, by then, written a number of plays and stories in addition to poetry, he had no great liking for the theatre; but he was increasingly drawn to painting and started reading books on art seriously. Perhaps I may have influenced him to join the art classes at the university and turn to oil painting. His preference was for abstract art. In the meantime, I had completed my studies, returned to Odisha and started looking for a job. Family circumstances compelled me to accept the first job that came my way and I took up a teaching position at Bargarh College. But JP proceeded unwaveringly along the path he had chosen for himself, joined the IAS, and came to Odisha as a young civil servant. It was during this early period in Odisha that he was attracted to the traditional pictorial art of the state and began researching the combination of culture and art in the Jagannath tradition. He was very active in bringing the arts that had been nurtured in the village of Raghurajpur to public attention, and was instrumental

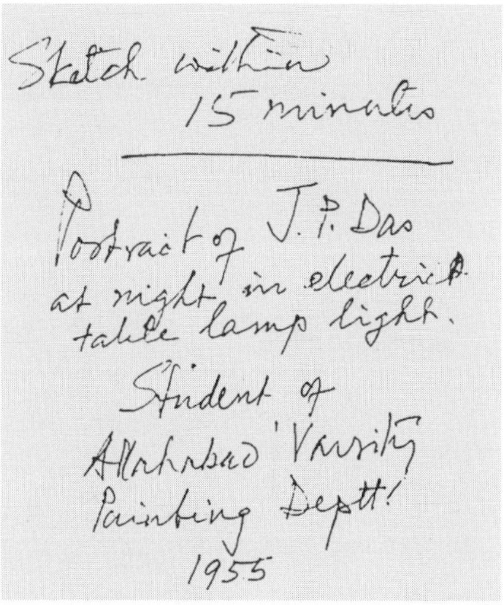

Sketch and note by Sarat Pujari

in making Raghurajpur famous around the world. As the place where Odishi and goti-pua dance had originated, as well as being the centre of pata chitra and fresco painting, Raghurajpur held great fascination for foreign visitors. For JP, with his many interests and talents, the transition from painting to dance and music, and further to theatre, was natural. When he moved to Delhi he had not only grown as a poet but also developed an interest in writing fictionalised history, which led to the creation of *Desha Kaala Paatra*, as well as drama. Had he remained

> in government service, he could not have contributed as much to the worlds of theatre, painting, literature, and poetry as he has been able to do. Fortunately for him, he had no family pressures and so was able to soar like a bird through regions of art. Apart from his graying hair, time has not affected him; he has remained a youth.

During the 6th and 7th decades of the 20th century, it was the dream of every student of the Humanities to get into the Indian Administrative Service. The IAS symbolised the ultimate in happiness, freedom, prosperity, and power. Those who entered the IAS constituted a class apart and considered themselves to be superior to the rest. This statement cannot, however, represent a universal truth; there were exceptions.

After his brilliant performance at the M.A. examination in Political Science in 1957, JP took up teaching and research at Allahabad University. Why then did he give up these occupations?

This is what his professor, Dr A.B. Lal has to say, 'Jagannath Prasad Das was among the brightest students of Utkal and Allahabad Universities. In my opinion, he would have made an ideal university professor. His entry into the Indian Administrative Service was a great loss to the world of education.'

At this time, many brilliant young Odias crossed over to the civil services after brief stints in university teaching. We do not know how much they profited professionally or financially thereby, but Odisha as well as the whole of India was certainly deprived of immense talent. I have often discussed informally with my IAS friends the reasons for their quitting the profession of teaching and found them inclined to avoid giving me a straight answer. In 1984, while I was a guest of the London-based artist Prafulla Mohanty, I met Lalitendu Mansingh. I asked Mr Mansingh, somewhat abruptly, 'Sir, why did you give up teaching to join the Indian Foreign Service? You could have become one of the country's leading political analysts if you remained in academics.' His brief reply was, 'Everyone wanted me to get into the IAS at the time, and so I did it.' Mansingh had topped the IAS examinations in 1966 and become famous overnight. Before that, he had been a Lecturer in Political Science at Utkal University. Subas Pani was a Lecturer in English at Utkal University before he was selected for the IAS while Ramakanta Rath, the poet, was a Lecturer in the same subject at Fakirmohan College, Balasore and Samar Ballabh Mohapatra taught English at Ramjas College, Delhi. Sitakanta Mohapatra, another renowned Odia poet, taught History at Ravenshaw College, Cuttack. I need not add to this list. Taking up a lectureship after the M.A. as a prelude to the Indian Administrative Service became the convention. This trend may perhaps represent the mentality of the younger generation and the social values of the time.

But JP's career represents an exception. He did enter the IAS in 1958 but resigned from the service in 1984. During an interview in Delhi with poet Keki Daruwala he was asked, 'Do you regret resigning from the IAS?' and JP's reply was, 'Yes, I regret the fact that I did not resign much earlier.'

At Allahabad, 1956

Could he have achieved what he has been able to achieve if he had not resigned? That is a debatable matter. Gopinath Mohanty, Ramakanta Rath, Sitakanta Mohapatra, and Haraprasad Das have been profoundly creative while remaining in service. Why could JP not have done it as well? But it is natural to believe that he preferred to shed the attractions of power and authority which the IAS confers. Some others in Odisha, admittedly few in number, have resigned from the administrative services, but in most cases the reason for resigning was their obtaining more lucrative employment elsewhere or entry into the world of politics or business. JP, on the other hand, has chosen to lead a life of freedom after resigning from the IAS.

At IAS Academy at Metcalfe House, New Delhi, 1958

Though JP did not become a teacher, he remained connected with the world of education. His research into painting, which we shall discuss later, is well known. During the 1990s, he was a member of the Syndicates of Utkal University as well as the University of Culture and helped to prepare the draft curriculum for the latter. When Noorul Hasan, the historian, was the governor of Odisha, JP was requested to assume the position of Vice-Chancellor of any one of the three oldest universities in Odisha—Utkal, Berhampur, or Sambalpur. Harekrushna Mahtab, the former Chief Minister of Odisha, had requested him to take over the editorship of the daily newspaper *Eastern Times*. Mrinal Sen, then Chairman of the Film Institute, had requested JP to be its Director. Even Mahesh Yogi had requested him to join the Transcendental Movement in some capacity. JP, however, was reluctant to accept any of these and chose to lead a free life.

In Delhi he got associated with some non-governmental organizations run by his friends. Among these Trees for Life, founded by his classmate from Allahabad, Balbir Mathur, and Manushi, founded by Madhu Kishwar deserve special mention.

We have discussed JP's life at Allahabad University and his foray into teaching and research; but perhaps we have digressed from our main concern. What about Jagannath Prasad Das, the writer? What were the poems, stories and plays he wrote at Allahabad? During this time, he had broadly distanced himself from literature and art although he studied literature deeply and retained his fascination for painting. This period appears to mark an interval in his creative life.

During the first part of the fifties, the silence of this young poet might have led some readers and critics to assume that for some reason he had said farewell to the world of literature. But the appearance of *Pratham Purush* in 1971 re-introduced them to the poet. But this was a very different poet, far more mature and explicit.

With wife Mitra, 1972

Kalahandi

As a member of the Indian Administrative Service, JP had to take on numerous assignments, both at the Centre and in Odisha, during 1958 to 1983. While the details of all these postings are not relevant, his emotional attachment to one place has become legendary – Kalahandi.

JP was Collector of Kalahandi from 1963 to 1966. Earlier, after completing his training at Metcalfe House, Delhi, he had been SDO, Panposh (1959–60) and Deputy Secretary in the Finance and Industry Departments, Government of Odisha (1961–63).

About 20 years after he left the place, JP wrote his poem 'Kalahandi'. This poem was translated into English as well as other Indian languages and is one of the better known poems in the world of Indian poetry. This is how the poem reads in English,

Kalahandi

Put away your maps
You do not need a helicopter to go there
Kalahandi is where starvation is

Indra brings no rain now
There are no more tender leaves on trees
The whole village is a cremation ground
The cracked earth and dry sand in river beds tell you

Facing page: *Sketch by Manish Barodia*

All projects have failed
The boundaries of poverty extend to infinity

You'll find Kalahandi wherever you look
In protruding ribs and staring eye sockets
Torn rags that no longer hide the body's shame
In pawned metal utensils
The gaping roofs of huts
The totality of two earthen pots

Kalahandi is everywhere
In the carnival of starving skeletons
The bazaars where children are auctioned
The sighs of young daughters
Being sold to brothels
The silent looks of peasants
Leaving their native soil
Take a still closer look at Kalahandi
In the emptiness of false reports
The crocodile tears of political speeches
Inflated statistics overflowing on stacks
And stacks of computer sheets
Cheap sympathy spewed out at conferences
The meaningless promises
Of government projects

Kalahandi is nearer than you think
In the momentary revolt of the tortured soul
The random sting of conscience
The rare regret of the inner being
Happy dreams turning into nightmares
In disease, hunger and helplessness
And the brooding possibility of bloodshed
How can we go into the prosperous safety
Of the twenty-first century leaving Kalahndi behind?

Few people had even heard of Kalahandi when JP became Collector of the district, but after the 1980s, Kalahandi became famous all over the world as a symbol of poverty, starvation, and suffering. Numerous writings on Kalahandi have appeared in English as well as in Odia. Among them are *The Politics of Hunger* (Macmillan, 2000) by John Carey, a friend of mine, who was then doing Ph.D. in Political Science from Hull University under Prof. Subrata Mitra, who hails from Odisha. John has visited Odisha several times and also knows Odia.

With Prabodh Kumar Sanyal, Bengali writer, 1964

Kalahandi was affected by an unprecedented drought in 1965–66, when JP was the Collector. A Collector has grave responsibilities at times such as these, although this is when bureaucrats tend to dodge these, hiding behind the shield of red tape. The help that reaches the starving people through the maze of bureaucratic procedures is negligible. But the J.P. Das we meet in 1965–66 does not represent the unfeeling bureaucracy; he comes across as a humanist, full of sympathy for the poor and suffering. One is reminded here of his left leanings as a student.

In 1966, JP met Prof. Sarbeshwar Das, his former teacher at Ravenshaw College and a well-known Gandhian thinker, at Kalahandi. This is what Prof. Das had to say of this meeting.

> I went to Kalahandi in 1966, where there was a drought and people were dying. Jagannath Das was the collector at Kalahandi while Ramakanta Mishra, another former student of mine, was collector at Bolangir. Rama Devi had already visited the place. I met JP and told him that starvation deaths had been reported in the newspapers. Such deaths were considered a serious matter even under the British administration. When Rama Devi reported,

after her visit, that people were dying of starvation, everyone felt aggrieved, particularly with the collector. It was only later that they realised what his constraints were. Communication was lacking. People were dependent on personal opinions expressed by village-level workers and doctors. There were many bureaucratic procedures to be followed. I came to understand the situation better after spending 15 days in Kalahandi. There were no roads. When I see the roads in Bhubaneswar today, I think of all the crores that the government is spending here. But what about other parts of Odisha?

... Jagannath toured the interior of Kalahandi for the next 15 days. Before I left for Balangir, Jagannath invited me home for a meal. Then, as we were chatting, Jagannath told me of all the obstacles he was facing. The telephones were not working. There were frequent reminders to send reports. The collector had to rely on subordinates, since he was not always able to reach interior places in time, although Jagannath did tour extensively.

Rasbihari, Behera, JP and Anup Singhdeo with Kalahandi football team, 1966

Prof. Sarbeswar Das remembers the pain of trying to help ordinary people despite bureaucratic hazards. He says that JP also experienced the helplessness of being unable to do what he wanted, despite his high position as collector of Kalahandi, and this could account for his decision to resign from the IAS. JP raised the issue himself at a session of the Meet the Author programme organised by the Sahitya Akademi in 2002.

> I consider the three years I spent in Kalahandi in a field job as Collector 40 years back as the most rewarding experience for me.... Orissa had gone through a famine a hundred years earlier in 1866, when a third of its population had perished, and people talked that it was going to happen again after a century. The 1866 famine was a man-made disaster, for the administration believed that there was enough food grain available in Orissa and refused to stop the export of grains or to bring grains into Orissa.
>
> In Kalahandi in 1965, by the middle of August it was felt that a scarcity situation was developing due to failure of rains. So I sent a report to Government telling that it was apprehended that sufficient rice cannot be procured to meet the food requirement this year if the dispatch of stocks from the various railheads of this district is not completely stopped. I have restricted movement of food grains outside the district and have also issued instructions to the railway stationmasters not to honour any indent for dispatch of stocks from Kalahandi.
>
> I will now read out a reply which said, 'I have no doubt that there is more rice in your district than you imagine and further that the crops of the current year will suffice for the year's supply. You must on no account interfere with legitimate trade.'
>
> Let me quickly add that the response I just read out was not addressed to me but to the Collector of Balasore who had made a similar request a hundred years

earlier, and the reply was sent to him by Commissioner Ravenshaw. I had come across the letter while researching for a book on 19th century Orissa.

The reply I got in 1965, a hundred years later, was a little more curt. It said, 'It has been decided to continue dispatches of rice from Kalahandi. The instructions issued to civil supplies staff and the railway authorities should be withdrawn forthwith.'

There was a complete failure of crops that year and by March 1966 the situation had become grave. In a report I made to the Government I gave the following facts to indicate how the situation had reached near-famine conditions, 'There is an abnormal increase in crimes; there are reports of starvation deaths; the general condition of health of the people has deteriorated and there is a high incidence of cases of malnutrition; cases of desertion of children have been reported; there is a heavy influx of beggars to towns and big villages in search of alms; families have deserted their villages in search of work elsewhere; free kitchens are attracting a large number of persons.

Gopal Mishra, well-known journalist, was a contemporary and childhood friend of JP's. Even now JP considers a visit to Bhubaneswar incomplete without meeting Gopal Mishra. Gopal Babu had met JP in Kalahandi during the famine. He writes,

The demands of my profession drove me to Kalahandi during the famine of 1965–66, when J.P. Das was the Collector. I met JP. The picture of Kalahandi which he presented before me, despite the constraints of his position, was quite enough for me. However, he had not expressed any personal opinion during his narrative. After conducting my own inquiries, I wrote in the newspaper, *Amrita Bazaar Patrika*, 'Kalahandi has been stricken by famine, not

FACING PAGE: *With Prime Minister Indira Gandhi in Kalahandi, 1966*

> drought'. The then Chief Minister, Late Sadashiv Tripathi, had read my article and called me for a discussion.

The account of the Kalahandi drought by Purna Chandra Hota, former Chairman of the Union Public Services Commission, provides valuable insights.

> In November 1963, J.P. Das was appointed Collector of Kalahandi, which was among the least developed districts in the country. In 1965, Kalahandi went through a severe drought. It was so severe that for the first time the Government of Odisha had to appoint a Special Relief Commissioner. The experienced and senior administrator V.S. Matthews was appointed to this post. J.P. Das and Mr Matthews toured the drought-affected areas. Drinking water was provided by deepening existing wells, and new wells dug along river beds. Old ponds and lakes were renovated. Free supplies of cooked food were provided in many places. The Collector was putting in 14 to 16 hours of hard work every day to cope with the situation.

JP never forgot Kalahandi after he left the place; nor has Kalahandi forgotten him. It is evident from a letter written to him by Anup Singhdeo, former MLA and former cabinet minister from Khariar.

Dear Sri Das,

I hope you remember me still. The people of Khariar have not forgotten you. Memories of your sincere services to the people during the famine of 1965–66 will always be cherished.

Anup Singhdeo
Khariar, 19.11.70

With wife Mitra, 1960

The experience of that famine seems to have pursued JP like a shadow, as revealed in his poem 'Kalahandi', written some 20 years later; or his description of the 'Nine-digit Famine' of Odisha in his novel *Desha Kaala Paatra,* or even his poem 'After Gujarat' (2003). And so it is that when we compare JP to many of his contemporaries, we find that his social awareness and involvement and his humanism give him a unique identity.

However, the stay in Kalahandi was a happy period in JP's personal and family lives. In 1960, he had married Mitra. She had distinguished herself as a singer, contemporary with renowned singers like Akshay Mohanty, Sikandar Alam, and Pranab Patnaik, prior to her marriage. She had participated in many cultural programmes at Ravenshaw College as well as the youth festival in Delhi. But her singing was almost forgotten after her marriage, though she did occasionally sing for her friends. However, many still remember her singing.

She worked for All India Radio as an Odia news reader after moving to Delhi with her husband. She has translated several books from English, Hindi, and Bengali to Odia, including *Neela Chand* (Hindi) and *Gosthabehari* (Bengali), published by the Sahitya Akademi and the National Book Trust, respectively.

An insightful glimpse into JP's life in Kalahandi has been provided by Rasbihari Behera, who knew JP intimately. In the years to come, Rasbihari Behera became a respected leader and was at one time a minister in the Congress government. In his words,

> I met Jagannath Prasad Das several times when he was Collector, Kalahandi, to discuss various programmes with him. Although he led a busy life as Collector, he was immensely interested in sports, especially tennis and was a skilled player of the game. It was through his efforts that a hard court came up on the Wheeler Club grounds in Kalahandi. As the number of players increased every day, flood-lighting had to be arranged to enable them to play at night. The Collector came punctually at 4.00 every afternoon to the Club to play, even when he was touring, after he had finished his work for the day.

In 1964

> The people of Kalahandi had been devastated by a series of droughts. Hundreds died in Khariar during the terrible drought of 1966, creating a stir that rocked the country. The sale of children by starving parents has become history. The then Prime Minister, Mrs Indira Gandhi, toured Kalahandi and saw for herself the suffering of the famine-stricken people of Khariar and Sonapali, which brought tears to her eyes. The youthful J.P. Das was the Collector. The Prime Minister took one look at him and asked the Revenue Divisional Commissioner, somewhat dubiously, 'Is this young man the Collector?' 'Yes, Madam,' was the confident reply.
>
> It is possible for youth to be courageous, industrious, and dedicated, as the young Collector proved through his

work. A great deal of assistance was received from foreign countries, and the Collector set all his subordinates to work, ensuring that the supplies reached those who were in need. His efforts were really praiseworthy.

Many journalists came to Kalahandi, and the photographs of the starving people published in newspapers created a sensation. Political parties tried to take advantage of the situation. The district administration organized meetings with the journalists and tried to counter the negative impressions that were being created.

The Collector personally helped countless farmers to get 'taccavi' loans from the government. His labours inspired his subordinates to carry out their duties with great sincerity, as a result of which the ordinary people benefited. The sports-loving J.P. Das was transformed, at this critical time, into a conscientious and dedicated official, for whom duty was prayer. A little negligence on his part could have been disastrous, but he was successful in bringing food to thousands of hungry mouths. That is why the people of Kalahandi cannot forget him.

ABOVE LEFT: *With Jaydeep Mukherjee, tennis player*

ABOVE: *Rourkela, 1960*

In Love with the Black Girl

'What a surprise! The Dark Girl is yours, I am sure. I love "it"'. This is what Mrinal Sen, the celebrated film director, wrote to JP on 7 Febraury 1973.

'Dark Girl' is a painting by JP, which was unveiled in Bhubaneswar in March 1971 at a solo exhibition of his paintings. By then, he had already acquired fame as a poet and administrator, but only a few intimate friends knew of his talent as a painter. That was the first and, unfortunately, the last exhibition of his paintings. He has painted rather few pictures, not more than 30 in all. For some reason, JP did not pursue his interest in painting. His friend Gopal Mishra says,

> I remember that one of his paintings had been hung up at the Bhubaneswar Club. It later disappeared. I was told subsequently that the Club had auctioned it away, along with some old furniture. I felt deeply pained. JP had been associated with the Club since its beginning and had helped in organizing its activities. He had donated his painting to the Club. It should have been our responsibility to preserve it.

JP had been attracted to painting since his childhood. His childhood friend, Muralidhar Satpathy, writes,

FACING PAGE: *The Dark Girl*

I remember Jagannath making a beautiful portrait of Pandit Madan Mohan Malaviya for publication in a hand-written magazine which the students of our class produced. That pencil-drawing came as a surprise to everyone. Apart from being the top student in the class, Jagannath was fond of writing short poems and drawing pictures.

The exhibition of paintings inaugurated in 1971 proved that after his brief exposure to art education at Allahabad University, JP had the potential to become a first rate artist, although he had no formal training. In the brochure that was produced on this occasion, the well-known artist Asit Mukherji wrote,

Not his first love —

By profession an administrator,
By training an intellectual
Sri J. P. Das is no tenderfoot
in painting ; this — his first
show will depict.

Self - taught as he is, Sri Das
also would prove himself
one among us.

The intuition by which Sri Das
took up the brush is also
dormant in most of us.

Let this venture instil a
confidence in seekers.

Asit Mukherjee
President, Silpisamsad, Bhubaneswar.

By profession, an administrator; by training, an intellectual. Painting may not be his first love, but he is no tenderfoot. Self-taught, he is still one of us. The intuition which made him take up the brush is dormant in most of us. Let this venture instil confidence in seekers.

Another well-known artist of the time, Asim Basu, narrates,

'I want to have an exhibition of my paintings', said J.P. Das, IAS. 'I've come to you to discuss how and where this can be done'. Surprised, I asked, 'Whose paintings did you say? Yours?' 'Yes', he replied. My surprise lingered. I had known some bureaucrats who wrote poetry, short stories, plays, or essays. But paintings? Who had ever heard of an IAS officer who painted? I looked at him in wonder, as a foreign tourist might look at a tribal inhabitant of Koraput. It was decided that our organization, Shilpi Sansad (artists' association) would sponsor the exhibition. Asit Mukherji and I went to JP's residence and selected the paintings to be exhibited.

In the Bhubaneswar of 1971, such an exhibition was a major event. Newspapers carried reports. This is how the *Prajatantra* of 9 March 1971, reported the event,

FACING PAGE: *Brochure of exhibition, 1971*

BELOW: *A poster of the painting exhibition, 1971*

Solo Exhibition of Paintings by Jagannath Prasad Das, Secretary, Works Department

Jagannath Prasad Das, a senior IAS officer of the state and Secretary, Civil Supplies Department, has distinguished

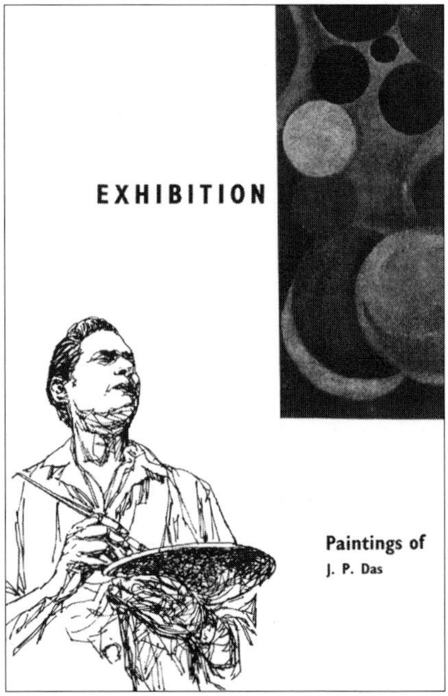

Invitation card for painting exhibition, 1973

himself as an outstanding amateur painter, as the exhibition of his paintings, inaugurated yesterday, clearly shows. No one suspected that he was a painter, but now no one can deny his talent as a painter.

This report focused on JP as an administrator and painter but made no mention of his literary achievements. This was not surprising, as his first volume of poems, *Pratham Purush*, had not yet been published by this time and *Stabaka*, the collection of short lyrics published in 1951, had not reached many readers.

What Dinanath Pathy, the well-known artist and writer and former President of the Odisha Lalit Kala Akademi had to say about JP's paintings is worth quoting,

> Jagannath Prasad Das began his journey of creation with poetry. After a few years, he entered the world of painting, and was able to wield brush and colours with deep interior emotion. The sixteen paintings exhibited

at Bhubaneswar were truly an expression of his great creative energy.

With Nityananda Kanungo, 1971

Indian Express reported thus, 'Most of these paintings bore no name or number, but some were mentioned by name. "Black Girl" is the most successful, though not all his paintings can be called successful. But a few of his paintings do establish him as an outstanding painter.' (*Indian Express*, March 1971).

JP has not said much about his paintings and does not seem inclined to do so even now. 'I have stopped painting; why talk about them?' he says. However, in an interview with Abhay Singh, he does give some useful insights into his incursions into the visual arts,

> It is difficult for a creative artist who attempts to express himself through different media to say which of them he finds easiest to use. Although my first exhibition of paintings preceded the publication of my first volume of poetry, I am unable to paint now for lack of time.

Since my efforts at creativity are confined to poetry and drama, I am reluctant to introduce myself as a painter and have said that poetry is my first love.

Each form of art has its own rules of expression. What canvas and paint are to painting, words are to poetry. Both media are dependent on technique. It is difficult to judge, using the criteria of art, which of these forms allows clearer expression. Lack of clarity indicates some deficiency in a poet or a painter. True, poetry appears at present to be the more dynamic medium for a variety of reasons such as the possibility of reaching a wider audience. Similarly, fiction and drama appear to be more dynamic than poetry.

I have been attracted to painting for a long time. But all I can say is that I studied painting briefly at Allahabad University during 1956–57. Both poetry and painting have limited roles to perform in transforming society. If any art can influence man even for a short time, or

With Mrinal Sen, Kolkata, 2000

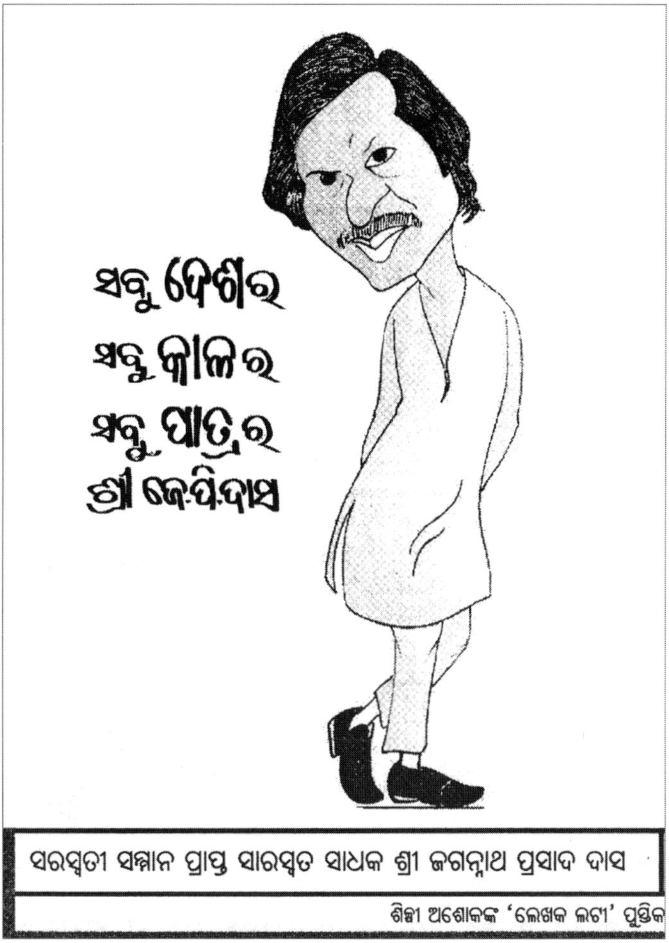

LEFT: *Cartoon by Silpee Ashok*

> after some delay, and compel him to think, I would consider it successful. Art is that which expresses both the internal and external form of mankind and society.

Whether JP paints again or not, Mrinal Sen is unlikely to forget the 'Dark Girl'. Those who have seen JP's paintings will surely acknowledge his talent as a painter.

Sehgal
1996

Puri Paintings

JP's book *Puri Paintings: The Chitrakaar and His Work* was published in 1982. It was a work of research, a crown-sized volume of about 200 pages in English, published simultaneously by Humanities Press in America and Arnold-Heinemann in India.

JP's reputation as a painter had been established by then. It is natural for a painter to engage in the study of painting. Nevertheless, many were taken by surprise when JP's scholarly work was published after painstaking research. This volume established JP's reputation as an art critic as well. Reviews were published in leading English newspapers in India and art critics abroad also took serious note of it.

FACING PAGE: *Sketch by Amar Nath Sehgal, 1996*

ABOVE: *With artist Jagannath Mahapatra, Raghurajpur, 1980*

There was an element of chance in the circumstances which turned J.P. Das, the poet, the dramatist, and the painter into an art historian. While serving in the Industries Department, Government of Odisha, he had studied the handicrafts of the state. During the sixties, he became interested in the patachitras (traditional paintings done on fabric) of Puri. Being a painter himself, he was fascinated by the traditional craft. It was linguist Prof. Debi Prasanna Patnaik who suggested that he continue his research as a Homi Bhabha Fellow and wrote to Dr Narayana Menon, a member of the Homi Bhabha Fellowships Council. JP was invited to Bombay for a discussion in which Prof Niharranjan Ray, famous art historian, also participated. JP was awarded the Homi Bhabha Fellowship in 1979.

During 1979–80, JP spent about eight months in Puri and Raghurajpur village, the home of patachitra. He also collected data from museums in Varanasi, London, and Ahmedabad and had long discussions with Prof Joanna Williams, well-known art historian at the University of Berkeley, California. Here is what JP said about his research project in an interview,

> Many years ago, art critic O.C. Ganguly had stated that although the arts and crafts of Odisha had been extensively studied, the traditional craft of patachitra had not received much scholarly attention. That was when I decided to undertake a study of Odishan painting. The patachitras of Odisha represent a living craft. My research involved a sociological study of chitrakaars (patachitra artists) as well as inquiry into patachitra techniques from an art-historian's perspective. Many distinguished chitrakaars have received national honours.

The senior artist, art-critic, and writer, Dinanath Pathy, has expressed his views on JP's paintings as well as his art-criticism on various occasions. He once told me, 'The book *Puri Paintings* is JP's greatest gift to Odisha.' Some might disagree with this view. They might think that his poetry, fiction, and other contributions to literature were his greatest achievements. As Dinanath is primarily a painter, one can understand his bias for *Puri Paintings*. Certainly this book gave a new direction to art criticism and history in Odisha, as everyone will agree.

During the 1970s and early 1980s, many art critics were interested in carrying on research into the plastic arts of Odisha,

With Joanna Williams

chiefly its sculpture, temple architecture, and painting. Eminent among them are Eberhard Fischer (Switzerland), Hermann Kulke (Germany), Joanna Williams, and Thomas E. Donaldson (both USA), and our own Kapila Vatsyayan, Sitakanta Mohapatra, Karuna Sagar Behera, and Subas Pani. One can also mention Dinanath Pathy's outstanding work on the pictorial arts of Odisha. When JP's book appeared in 1982, none of the scholars named above had published the findings of their research. In 1983, Subas Pani and I visited Raghurajpur, the chitrakaars' village near Puri. It had not then gained the international fame that it has acquired since. I was not aware of the book which JP had published a year before, although Subas Pani might have been.

Nearly every inhabitant of Raghurajpur was an artist; most of them were chitrakaars, while others made wooden images of the three deities in the temple at Puri, wooden toys representing animals, or masks. The village is only a short distance from Chandanpur. One can drive straight into the village in a jeep, although the condition of the road makes this a little unsafe. Speaking to the villagers gave me the impression that they were quite used to interacting with government officials and visitors from the city. Economically, they appeared fairly stable. They did not merely follow traditional themes and techniques but were also willing to experiment.

JP's *Puri Paintings* contains 13 chapters. The description of the painters of the past, found in archival records, has been salvaged. There is also a discussion of the close relationship between Odia literature and the patachitra tradition. The 13 chapters present a narrative of the environment in which painters live and work, their caste and class divisions, the 36 *niyogs* (associations of *sevayats* [servants of the Lord] in the Jagannath temple), the *sevas* (services to the Lord) offered by the painters, the evolution of the patachitra tradition, its decline and revival and a description of the materials and techniques used.

Prof. Sumanyu Satapathy of Delhi University wrote, 'The book is a remarkable blend of research and story-telling. It is eminently readable and addressed to Indian as well as international audiences and completely free from any parochial bias.'

In his research, JP brought together the accounts left behind by many historians and art critics such as Andrew Sterling, James

With Haati Maharana, Puri, 1981

With Chitrakars in Raghurajpur, 1981

Ferguson, W.W. Hunter, Manmohan Ganguly, Alice Boner, Stella Kramrisch, D.P. Ghosh, and O.C. Ganguly. JP spent months among the chitrakaars, talking to them about their craft. This gives to his narrative a certain liveliness as well as authenticity. The patachitra tradition comes alive through his book.

There have been extensive reviews of *Puri Paintings* by international critics. Here is a brief excerpt from an exhaustive review by Eberhard Fischer.

> The approach of JP Das is unusual for an Indian art historian; it is interdisciplinary, partly ethnographic sociological, partly art historical. This is an extremely useful form of documentational research, as the still existing but waning living tradition of Indian artists sheds light on their history, making all historic reconstruction models more (likely) understandable.'

Patachitra and other traditional forms of Odishan art as well as the village of Raghurajpur have undoubtedly achieved great prominence after the publication of *Puri Paintings*. The well-known artist from Raghurajpur, Jagannath Mohapatra, was awarded the D.Litt. degree by Utkal University in 1997, and another artist, Ananta Maharana, from Dandasahi, a village near Raghurajpur, received the highest national award for arts and crafts in 2003.

Anasara Pati procession, Puri, 1981

JP's next publication was *Chitrapothi: Illustrated Palm-leaf Manuscripts from Orissa* (1985). Next to appear was *Palm Leaf Miniatures: The Art of Raghunath Prusty of Orissa* (1991), which JP co-authored with Joanna Williams.

In *Chitrapothi* JP states how illustrations are made on palm-leaf manuscripts, mainly of kavya texts. It is a traditional Odishan craft, but not many are acquainted with this art form. Eighteenth century was the golden age of Odia Poetry, and this was when many illustrated palm leaf manuscripts were created.

Chitrapothi runs to 130 pages and is divided into 15 chapters. It presents a number of poetic compositions and illustrations based on them.

Palm Leaf Miniatures, the other volume, is an account of the life and work of the 19th century artist Raghunath Prusty, who had been based in Ganjam. Such a work on a traditional illustrator of palm leaf manuscripts had not been presented before to readers at the national level. The author's intentions were to prove that Raghunath Prusty was a great artist; to highlight the unique character of traditional Odishan paintings;

ABOVE: *JP being received by Chief Justice of India, K.G. Balakrishnan and others, Poetry Reading at Supreme Court Bar Association, 2007*

and to focus on the social background against which Odishan painting evolved.

All these three much-discussed books by JP appeared during 1982–1991. The last two may be called extensions of *Puri Paintings*. These books established JP as a leading art historian. It was hoped that JP would continue his work as an art historian, but that was not to be. In a conversation with Dinanath Pathy he said, 'I have done quite a bit of art criticism; I would now like to concentrate on creative literature.'

It may not be irrelevant here to say that there is no dividing line between research and creative work. Unless a researcher is creative, his work is likely to be insipid – mere assemblage. So too, the work of a creative writer or artist is likely to be feeble unless he or she has the mind of a researcher. Just as *Puri Paintings* reveals a creative flair, the novel *Desha Kaala Paatra* shows the dedication of a researcher.

Theatre, Stage, and Cinema

While being posted at Cuttack as Director of Industries, JP was in close touch with Ananta Mahapatra, Rabindra Nath Das, Hemanta Das, and Dr Madhusudan Khadanga. Ananta was a reputed actor as well as theatre director; Rabindra was Director, All India Radio, Cuttack while actor Hemanta had been JP's classmate at Christ College. In 1972, an amateur play group, Srujani, staged Manoranjan Das' play *Amrutasya Putra* (the child of immortality), under Ananta Mahapatra's direction. After the play was staged, JP wrote a review

FACING PAGE: *Sketch by Amrish, 1984*

With Biswanath Das, Harihara Mahapatra, Jadunath Das Mahapatra and Babulal Doshi at Kala Vikash Kendra, 1972

in the magazine *Enact*, published from Delhi. He also reviewed several other Odia plays, including Bijay Mishra's *Dui ti Surya-dagdha Phulanku nei* (concerning two Sun-blanched flowers).

These reviews marked JP's formal entry into the world of Odia theatre. Ananta Mahapatra, who was then directing radio plays for All India Radio, suddenly asked JP one evening, 'Why don't you write a radio play?' Perhaps JP was unable to evade this request from a friend, and went on to write not one but a number of radio plays, which are lost and forgotten today, although it may still be possible to retrieve them from All India Radio's archives. However, his radio play *Kaacha Ghara* (the glass house), which highlighted the problems and restlessness of the student community, had been widely discussed.

It was not as though JP had shown no interest at all in theatre prior to 1972, but he had not given it much importance, being absorbed in poetry and painting. However, the one act play *Janey Janaka Paayin* (one for the other) written by him was staged at the Cuttack Club, thanks mainly to the enthusiasm of Ananta Mahapatra. JP himself was among the cast, which also included Ananta Mahapatra, Capt. Ananta Mohanty, Mitra Das (JP's wife), and a gentleman named Subramaniam who knew no Odia and so was required to speak just one word of dialogue, 'acchha' (very well).

There is no strong tradition in Odisha of playwrights directing plays or acting on the stage. However, Jaganmohan Lala, the first Odia playwright, who had organised his own theatre group Radhakanta Rangamancha in Mahanga, near Cuttack, presented the members of his own family in different female as well as male roles in his play *Babaji* (the mendicant). The pioneer Baishnab Pani was simultaneously writer, director, music composer, as

TOP: *As Fateh Mohammad* in Bakshi Jagabandhu

FACING PAGE TOP: Made for Each Other, *1972. JP second from left*

FACING PAGE BOTTOM: *With Ananta Mahapatra, Mona Das, and Madhusudan Khadanga, 1987* well as an actor for his own operatic plays. This was true also of Kalicharan Patnaik. Although JP, unlike the dramatists just named, did not have an extended relationship with the theatre, he too was actively involved in acting and stage management. In the historical play *Bakshi Jagabandhu*, written by Manoranjan Das, he had enacted the role of Fateh Mohammad when the play was produced in Delhi in 1978. He probably had not imagined then that Fateh Mohammad would become a prominent character in his novel *Desha Kaala Paatra* (the time, place, and the characters), written 20 years later.

Apart from writing plays and acting in them, JP was intimately associated at the time with the theatre movement in Cuttack. Manoranjan Das, the leading Odia dramatist, wrote,

> Some friends of ours encouraged us greatly through their presence at rehearsals of the play *Amrutasya Putra*, staged by Srujani in 1972, which ran late into the night. I specially remember two of them: one was J.P. Das, the young I.A.S. officer who later became known as a poet, playwright and painter, and the other Dr Madhusudan Khadanga, the well-known surgeon.

Over the years, JP wrote five plays, including *Suryasta Purbaru* (before the sunset) (1970), *Sabaa Sesha Loka* (the underdog) (1978), *Asangata Natak* (the absurd drama) (1981), *Purbaraag* (early love) (1985), and *Sundardas* (1994). He has published no other play since.

JP's output in this field is not large. Before we comment on his work as a playwright, it will be appropriate to review the state of Odia theatre then. Modern drama / stage-acting began with Jaganmohan Lala's *Babaji* (1877), although farcical and musical plays had existed earlier. To an extent, Mohansundar Debagoswami had modernised the ancient rasa leela genre. Subsequently, Kalicharan Patnaik, whose Odisha Theatres, Annapurna Theatre (A and B Groups), and Janata Theatre that marked the advent of professional theatre in Odisha, regularly presented mythological as well as social plays

Dishantar

presents an Oriya play
by J. P. Das
Translated into Hindi by Kanti Deb
Directed by Ram Gopal Bajaj

Suryastak

पात्र / cast

दीपंकर / Deepankar	ओम पुरी / Om Puri
संजय / Sanjay	सुदेश स्याल / Sudesh Syal
शीला / Sheela	वेद सिन्हा / Ved Sinha
सरोज / Saroj	माला मेहरोत्रा / Mala Mehrotra

निर्देशन **राम गोपाल**
Direction **Ram Gopal**

मंच / Stage	सुदेश स्याल / Sudesh Syal
प्रकाश योजना / Lighting	आर० के० ढींगरा / R.K. Dhingra
वेश / Costumes	वेद सिन्हा / Ved Sinha
संगीत चयन / Music Selected by	कौशल / Kaushal
प्रस्तुति नियन्त्रण / Production	बी० पी० सिन्हा / B.P. Sinha

Oriya play

NEW DELHI. Oct. 14 (PTI)—The Oriya Samaj of Delhi today presented "Buxi Jagabandhu", a historical play, as part of the Kumar Utsav celebrations.

The play, based on the book by Mr Manoranjan Das, portrayed the fiery life of Buxi Jagabandhu who led the revolt against the British rule in Orissa in 1817.

The play, directed by Mr Jatin Das, included J. P. Dass, Shyam Mahapatra and Nirupma Tripathi in the cast.

A Kumar Purnima dance was staged before the start of the play.

ABOVE LEFT: *An announcement of the play,* Suryastak

ABOVE: *A report in the* Times of India, *New Delhi, 15 October 1978*

until the 1950s. Baishnab Pani founded his own theatre group and staged operas written by himself to audiences outside as well as within Odisha. Ashwini Kumar Ghosh, Kalicharan Patnaik, Gopal Chhotray, Kartik Chandra Ghosh, Ramchandra Misra, Bhanjakishore Patnaik, and Manoranjan Das presented plays on the professional stage. Audiences bought tickets to witness them and actors and other stage artists earned their livelihood through these plays. Apart from these plays by professional groups, almost every college in Odisha staged a complete play each year, under the auspices of its drama society, before large audiences. This was considered an important part of student activities.

Professional Odia theatre went into decline after the 1970s and 1980s, possibly because of the advent of cinema and television. Theatre was replaced by *Jatra* (village opera) and *Melody* (stage shows by professional musicians). *Jatra* did not encourage the development of social or historical plays written by eminent playwrights; instead, it was turned into cheap entertainment.

THEATRE—'79

presents

J. P. Das's

SUBH TON HETHLA AADAMI

(UNDERDOG)

(A Panjabi Version of Oriya Play)

Direction : WARYAM MAST

Translation : Vats Madan Mohan

at Tagore Theatre, Chandigarh

on 2nd August 1982

at 7-00 P.M. (Sharp)

The success of *Suryasta Purbaru* nationally was an achievement not only for JP but for Odia theatre as well. No Odia play or playwright had been so widely acclaimed earlier. Here is an excerpt from the review published in the Calcutta edition of *Hindustan Standard*, 17 June 1972 under the heading 'Healthy Sign'.

> It is a healthy sign that Calcutta's theatre groups are being forced by necessity to look beyond the borders of the state for good plays in other Indian languages for production in Bengali. Recently we saw two very successful experiments in this field. One was a Marathi play with the Bengali title *Chop Adalat Cholche* and another an Oriya play *Suryaster Aage* written by the young poet, painter, and playwright Jagannath Prasad Das. The latter play was produced by Theatre Guild with great success. Incidentally, this was the first play written by the author, the first Oriya play in Bengali staged in this city, and the first, anywhere perhaps, staged in translation before the original has been produced.

FACING PAGE TOP LEFT: *Announcement of play in Punjabi, 1979*

FACING PAGE TOP RIGHT: Suryasta Purbaru *in Bangla, Calcutta, 1972*

FACING PAGE BOTTOM: *With Director Shyamal Sen and cast of* Suryasta Purbaru, *1972*

BELOW: *With Ustad Amir Khan, Begum Akhtar, Minati Mishra and others, Cuttack Music Circle, 1970.*

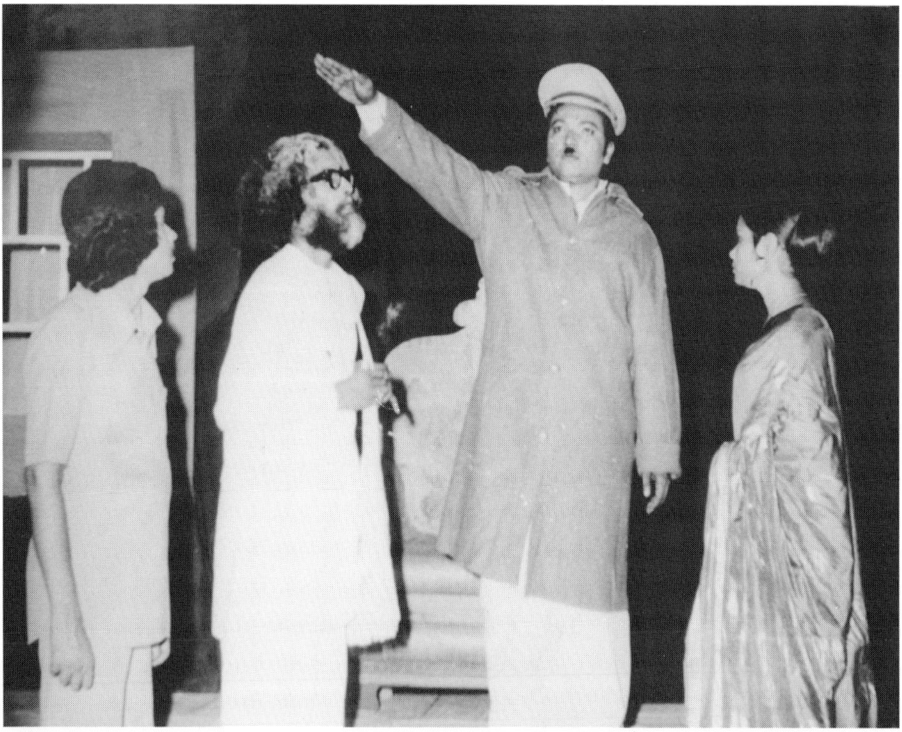

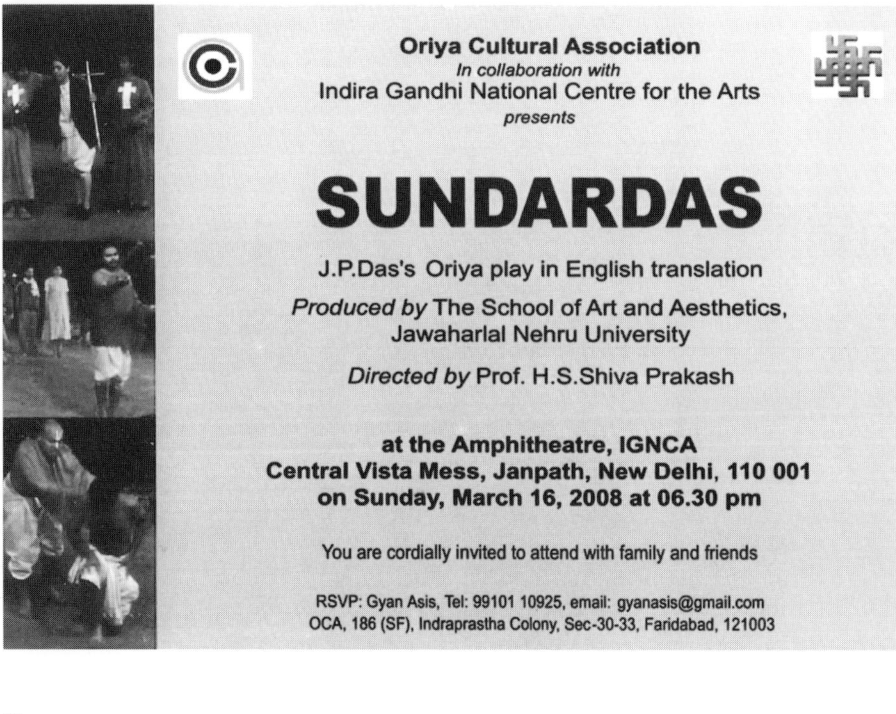
Oriya Cultural Association
In collaboration with
Indira Gandhi National Centre for the Arts
presents
SUNDARDAS
J.P.Das's Oriya play in English translation
Produced by The School of Art and Aesthetics,
Jawaharlal Nehru University
Directed by Prof. H.S.Shiva Prakash
at the Amphitheatre, IGNCA
Central Vista Mess, Janpath, New Delhi, 110 001
on Sunday, March 16, 2008 at 06.30 pm
You are cordially invited to attend with family and friends
RSVP: Gyan Asis, Tel: 99101 10925, email: gyanasis@gmail.com
OCA, 186 (SF), Indraprastha Colony, Sec-30-33, Faridabad, 121003

FACING PAGE TOP: *Asim Basu in the play* The Underdog

FACING PAGE BOTTOM: *Announcement on the staging of* Sundardas, *2008*

LEFT: *With Ram Gopal Bajaj, 2001*

The next two plays by JP, after *Suryasta Purbaru* and *Saba Sesha Loka* were *Asangata Natak* and *Purbaraag* which do not seem to have been equally successful in arousing the interest of audiences. *Asangata Natak* was staged in Bhubaneswar under Dheera Mallik's direction.

However, JP's last play *Sundardas* was a valuable contribution to Odia theatre, although it does not appear to have been given the importance it deserves. It has a cast of 30 characters, chief among whom are Sadhu Sundardas, Reverends Lacey, Sutton, and Bampton. The play is about religious conversion by Christian missionaries in Odisha in the early 19th century and its reaction on Hindu society. The English translation was done by Paul St-Pierre, Lilawati Mohapatra, and K.K. Mohaptra. In his Preface, Prof. St-Pierre writes, 'The play gives reality to the conflicting world views in contact in this meeting of Christianity and Hinduism in the context of empire, subjugation, and colonization. The play illustrates the problematic nature of conversion, insofar as it implies the rejection of one's past and the adoption of a new identity.'

Two modern plays were presented in 2007 by the School of Arts and Aesthetics at Jawaharlal Nehru University, *Sundardas* and *Jaat hi Puchcho Sadhu ki* by Marathi playwright Vijay Tendulkar. JP's play was directed by H.S. Shivaprakash. In the context of the controversy that had been sparked off by religious conversion in recent years, the play became very topical.

Although JP has written no new plays after 1984, his links with the world of theatre have remained unbroken. This is what Asim Basu, successful director of several Odia plays, had to say in this connection, 'J.P. Das is a playwright. I cannot remember now whether I had acted in his play *Saba Sesha Loka* before or after forming part of the audience for *Suryasta Purbaru*. But even today, I cannot forget the following dialogue from the play,

FACING PAGE TOP: *With Gulzar, 2015*

FACING PAGE BELOW LEFT: *A letter from Gulzar, 2001*

FACING PAGE BELOW RIGHT: *Children's Film Festival, Bhubaneswar, 1987*

BELOW: *With Ram Gopal Bajaj and Rudraprasad Sengupta, Bhubaneswar, 2008*

BELOW RIGHT: *Shooting for telefilm Sunaina, 1985*

Wife:	Bapi has written a letter; won't you read it?
Husband:	You've read it, haven't you? That's enough.
Wife:	Why won't you read it?
Husband:	Because it wasn't written by Bapi. The English teacher in the Public School writes out model letters on the blackboard and the boys merely copy them and send them to Mummy and Daddy.

How easily and in how few words does J.P. Das point his finger at a particular social class!

Here is a piece of dialogue, equally charged with dialectic, from another play *Asangata Natak*.

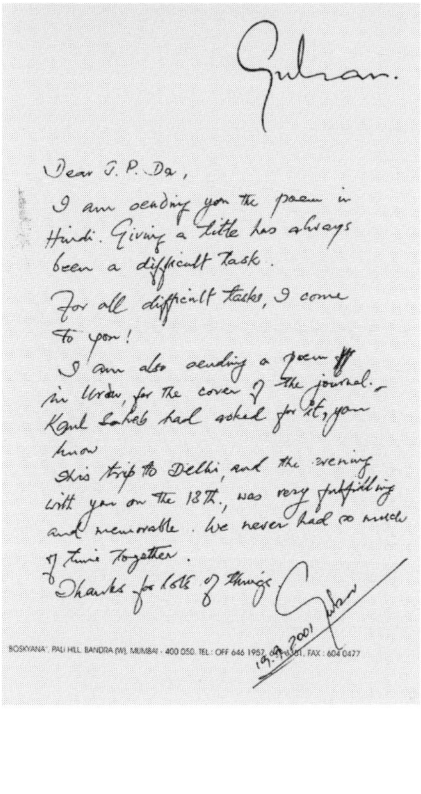

Gulzar.

Dear J. P. Da,

I am sending you the poem in Hindi. Giving a title has always been a difficult task.

For all difficult tasks, I come to you!

I am also sending a poem in Urdu, for the cover of the journal. Kaul Sahab had asked for it, you know

This trip to Delhi, and the evening with you on the 18th., was very fulfilling and memorable. We never had so much of time together.

Thanks for lots of things.

Gulzar

19.9.2001

BOSKYANA', PALI HILL, BANDRA (W), MUMBAI - 400 050. TEL.: OFF 646 1957, [illegible], FAX : 604 0477

First man What time is it?
Second man: Twelve minutes.
First man Twelve minutes past what?
Second man: My watch doesn't have an hour hand.
First man: Then you didn't tell me the correct time.
Second man: Why not? If I had said twelve minutes past eight, would that have been correct? I couldn't have told you how many macro seconds and nano seconds after that! In which case, twelve minutes after eight isn't the correct time either.

> Such lines are not easily forgotten. Our group, Ebam Amey (and we), had recently staged the play *Tata Niranjana* by Bijy Mishra and was looking for a new play, when we came across *Sabaa Sesha Loka*. I entrusted Dheera Mallik with the direction of the play and chose to act in it instead. Here, JP has tried to show, through the character of the professor which I played, how human personality becomes hostage to power. It seemed to reflect my own personality, for had I not given up my government job in order to escape this fate? And JP? Did he too resemble the professor? Else why should he have given up his job? Such thoughts came to me repeatedly.

JP has been a trustee of the Odisha Rangamancha Trust as well as a member of the Executive Committee of the National School of Drama. He has toured Sweden and Russia as a prominent member of the International Theatre Group and has studied the theatre movements in these countries.

Here one could also mention JP's connection with the world of cinema. He was connected with the Delhi Film Society and was a member of the Executive Committee of the Children's Film Society of India along with renowned lyricist Gulzaar. He and Gulzaar have been close friends for many years. He presided over the Jury

LEFT ABOVE: *Presiding over the Jury of the Children's Film Festival of India, Bangalore, 1985*

LEFT: *Jaya Bachchan and others, International Children's Film Festival of India, New Delhi, 1989. JP, fourth from left*

of the International Festival of Children's Films in Bangalore in 1985. A festival of Children's Films was organized in Bhubaneswar in 1987, thanks mainly to his efforts. JP collaborated with actor director Amol Palekar in organizing this film festival. He also edited a volume entitled *Films for Children,* published in 1987. He was a jury member of the International Children's Film Festival held in Delhi in 1989 and was a member of the jury for the International Children's Film Festival held in Abo, Finland, in 1990.

राष्ट्रीय
फिल्म विकास निगम
लिमिटेड
भारत सरकार का उद्यम
शिव सागर इस्टेट, 'डी' ब्लाक,
डा. ॲनी बेसंट रोड, वरली,
बम्बई-400 018.

NATIONAL
FILM DEVELOPMENT
CORPORATION
LIMITED
A GOVERNMENT OF INDIA ENTERPRISE
Shiv Sagar Estate, 'D' Block
Dr. Annie Besant Road worli
Bombay-400 018.

NFDC

TELEX : 011- 5700 NFDC IN
PHONE : 372393 • 372394 • 379096 • 379842

Ref: NFDC/CH/ 3937 /84

March 8, 1984.

HRISHIKESH MUKHERJEE
CHAIRMAN

Thank you for your letter dated February 13, 1984. I was away in West Bengal and Orissa to discuss various matters with the respective State Film Development Corporations. Hence the delay in reply.

I am thankful to you for suggesting the name of Shri Surendra Mohanty which I have already conveyed to Directorate of Film Festivals.

I also thank you for your latest book which after reading I will write to you again.

With love,

Yours

Hrishida

(HRISHIKESH MUKHERJEE)

Dr. J.P. Das,
226, West Kidwai Nagar,
New Delhi 110 023.

hm/vsk

Jaya Bachchan
'Pratiksha', 10th North-South Road, Juhu-Parle Scheme, Bombay-400 049

6th July, 1988.

Dear Dr. Das,

Thank you, very very much for standing by, so strongly in our support.

My C. F. S. I. colleagues and I felt a lot stronger with you and your co-operation.

Have a super holiday, my best wishes to your daughter and son-in-law.

With warmest regards.

Yours sincerely,

Jaya

(JAYA BACHCHAN)

What did you think of the Stories?

RIGHT ABOVE: *Letter from Hrishikesh Mukherjee, Chairman, NFDC*

RIGHT: *Letter from Jaya Bachchan, Chairperson, CFSI*

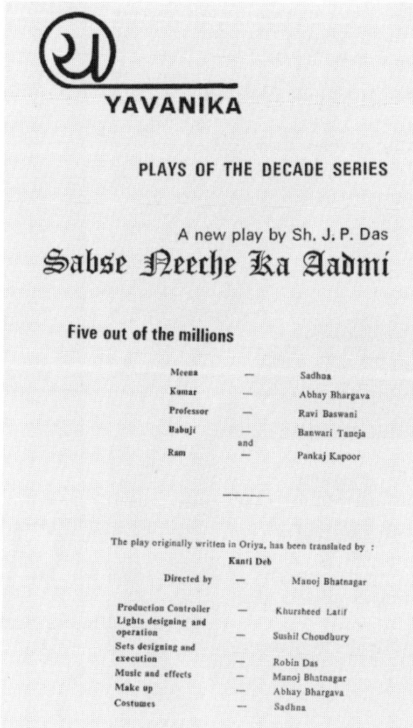
YAVANIKA

PLAYS OF THE DECADE SERIES

A new play by Sh. J. P. Das

Sabse Neeche Ka Aadmi

Five out of the millions

Meena	—	Sadhna
Kumar	—	Abhay Bhargava
Professor	—	Ravi Baswani
Babuji	—	Banwari Taneja
	and	
Ram	—	Pankaj Kapoor

The play originally written in Oriya, has been translated by :

Kanti Deb

Directed by — Manoj Bhatnagar

Production Controller	—	Khursheed Latif
Lights designing and operation	—	Sushil Choudhury
Sets designing and execution	—	Robin Das
Music and effects	—	Manoj Bhatnagar
Make up	—	Abhay Bhargava
Costumes	—	Sadhna

JP is friends with several celebrated movie actors and directors, including the late Hrishikesh Mukherjee, Mrinal Sen, Rabi Ghosh, and Jaya Bachchan.

ABOVE LEFT: *Announcement of* Sabse Neeche Ka Aadmi

ABOVE: *With Bhupen Hazarika during Children's Film Festival, Thiruvananthapuram, 1991*

The yawning gap

When at a recent meeting of the Janata Parliamentary Party Union Cabinet Minister Biju Patnaik painted a rosy picture of the present situation in the country, Prof. Dilip Chakravarty, MP, chose to recite poetry to contradict him and bring out the gap between expectations and achievements. Prof. Chakravarty was quoting from J. P. Das's book of poems: "First Person," and the poem: "Homecoming." The lines were:

When I left home
I thought of taking some colour
and light from the sky;
some heat from the sun,
roar from the clouds
thrill from the woods,
and some experience from the void.

I got nothing.
So I thought of taking
some hope from the sky,
promise from the sun
and dream from the clouds,
some surprise from the void.
I lost my way.
In my helpless return,
I sit and wonder
about fate's injustice;
looking at the lines on my palms
I measure the distance
between one despair and another.

Coincidentally the poet is also from the Minister's home state (Orissa).

meet a poet

IT WAS AN ODD PLACE FOR READing poetry—a corner of a Park Street restaurant jampacked with the Saturday evening crowd. But thus we escaped notice which we wanted; the animated chatter droned on and glasses and china clinked—a fascinating counterpoint to the melodious chanting of some Oriya poems by the poet himself, Jagannath Prasad Das from Bhubaneswar. For Bengalis like us (or should we say Indian Bengalis now?) the language was no barrier; not one word failed to ring a bell; and the unfamiliar sound of case-endings and inflexions of verbs did not distract us from our view of the poet's chairoscuro world where the melancholy of unrequited or perhaps unrealizable love is too deep to be relieved by the half lights of dream or purposeful quest. The agony was muted and a civilized sadness expressed with frosty elegance lent great beauty to most of the poems. No wonder the repository of these poems, J.P.'s first book, *Prathama Purusha* (First Person), also printed in a striking format with an excellent cover design (Lark Books, Cuttack-2. Price Rs. 4), should be a best seller. And our grilling of this young and very modest poet produced a surprise—he is also a painter, playwright and top civil servant in the Orissa Government! "How do you find time to cultivate your private passions," we asked. "I get up before sunrise and squeeze a couple of hours for myself out of my busy routine," he said. So, the popular image of a poet being a slothful late-riser is all wrong!

And this reminds us. How good it would have been if the languages of India demolished their own and impenetrable walls of alphabets and adopted a common script ! At least half the battle for integration would have been won.

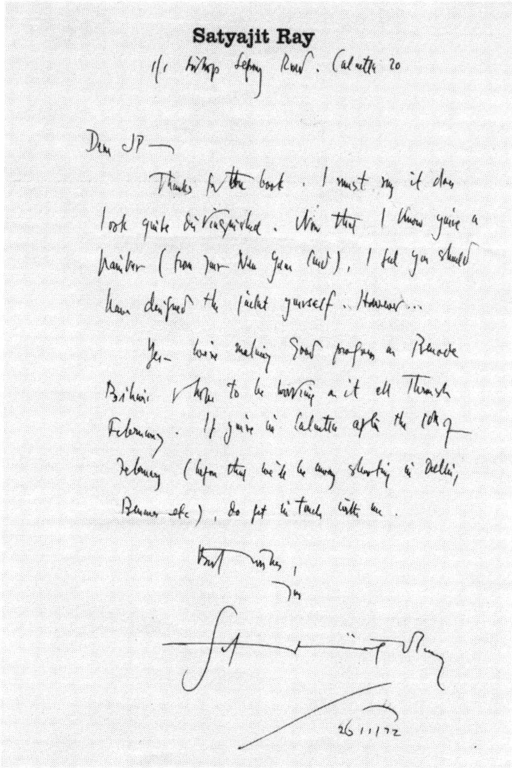

Satyajit Ray
1/1 Bishop Lefroy [illegible]. Calcutta 20

Dear JP—

Thanks for the book. I must say it does look quite distinguished. Now that I know you're a painter (from your New Year card), I feel you should have designed the jacket yourself.. However...

Yes — we're making good progress on [illegible] [illegible] & hope to be working on it all through February. If you're in Calcutta after the 10th of February (before that we'll be away shooting in Delhi, Bombay etc), do get in touch with me.

Best wishes,
Yours
Satyajit Ray
26.11.72

LEFT: *Letter from Satyajit Ray*

FACING PAGE LEFT: *A report in the* National Herald, *New Delhi, 3 November 1978*

FACING PAGE RIGHT: *The report in the* Hindustan Standard, *Kolkata, 28 February 1972*

> believe that Satyajit Ray had designed the cover and actor Ananta Mahapatra had published it. It was my first publication, though not the last.

The printer of the book, Dibakar Mishra, writes,

> *Pratham Purush* was printed at our Goswami Press in 1971. The author insisted on high quality paper and error-free printing. The book was composed with great care on a machine we had just imported from London and printed on a German machine. Binders had been brought from Calcutta to ensure good binding. Jagannath Babu's interest in the process of book production, at a time when most buyers of books seemed unaware of its importance, gave me great joy.

Odia poetry was beginning to take a new turn when *Pratham Purush* appeared. The influence of Sachi Routray had not waned but Guruprasad Mohanty's *Kaala Purush* (the man of the time) and *Nutan Kavita* (new poetry) as well as Ramakanta Rath's *Kete Dinara* (of many days) had sounded the advent of a new epoch, and JP's *Pratham Purush* was another landmark.

Like *Suryasta Purbaru*, JP's first play, *Pratham Purush* was acclaimed nationally, marking a major achievement for Odia poetry. An evening of poetry reading was organised in Calcutta in 1972 in honour of JP, at which the famous Bangla poet Shakti Chattopadhyay was present, among others. Here is a report which the English daily *Hindustan Standard* carried on this event on 28 February 1972 under the heading 'Meet a Poet', which is worth quoting at length.

> It was an odd place for reading poetry—a corner of a Park Street restaurant jam-packed with the Saturday evening crowd. But thus we escaped notice which we wanted; the animated chatter droned on and glasses

In 1972

> and china clinked—a fascinating counterpoint to the melodious chanting of some Oriya poems by the poet himself, Jagannath Prasad Das from Bhubaneswar. For Bengalis like us (or should we say Indian Bengalis now?) the language was no barrier; not one word failed to ring a bell. And the unfamiliar sound of case endings and inflexions of verbs did not distract us from our view of the poet's chiaroscuro world, where the melancholy of unrequited or perhaps unrealizable love is too deep to be relieved by the half lights of dream or purposeful quest. The agony was muted and a civilised sadness expressed with frosty elegance lent great beauty to most of the poems.

The 'melancholy of unrequited love' and the 'half lights of dream and purposeful quest' pervaded JP's next ten collections of poems as well. Perhaps it was the hazards of city life that made the Bangla audience in Calcutta so responsive to *Pratham Purush*. The refinement, transparency, and spontaneity of the poems in *Pratham Purush* are preserved in the collections of poems that followed.

Pratham Purush was translated into Hindi in 1974 while JP's friend, Prof. Deba Patnaik translated it into English in the same year. Odia poets contemporary to JP included Ramakanta Rath and Sitakanta Mohapatra. In his book *Odia Sahityara Kramavikash* (the evolution of Odia literature), the novelist-critic Surendra Mohanty has provided some valuable insights into the work of these three poets. Of JP he says,

> Jagannath Prasad could have been one of the leading poets of the seventies, but his talents were extended into fields as diverse as painting and drama. He is also a member of the Indian Administrative Service. Apart from *Pratham Purush*, no other collection of his poems has been published. Although these poems reflect the

> contemporary sense of rootlessness, isolation, and loss of self-identity, they are free from the affectations and experimentalism of new poetry.

That comment by Surendra Mohanty deserves notice. His book was published in 1978, while JP's second volume of poems, *Anya Sabu Mrityu* (other deaths) had already been published in 1976. Apparently, Surendra Mohanty was not aware of it. He might have feared that a talented poet like Jagannath Prasad would turn away from poetry, and that is why he termed JP an 'unrealised promise'. In fact, JP devoted himself almost exclusively to poetry during these years and received the Kendra Sahitya Akademi award for *Aahnik* (diurnal rights) in 1990 and the Saraswati Samman for *Parikrama* (the circuit) in 2007. The collections of poems that followed *Pratham Purush* included *Anya Sabu Mrityu (the other deaths) (1976), Je Jaahaara Nirjanataa* (each to his own solitude) (1979), *Anya Desha Bhinna Samay* (another land, another time) (1982), *Jaatrara Pratham Pada* (the first leg of the journey) (1988), *Aahnik* (1990), *Sthira Chitra* (still life) (1991), *Sacharaachara* (the universe), *Smritira Sahara* (the city of memories) (1995), *Parikrama* (1998), and *Asamay* (the wrong time) (2004).

Many senior as well as young critics have commented on JP's poetry. In his preface to *Shabdabheda* (1981), Hindi translation of a collection of poems by JP, Ramakanta Rath writes, 'Jagannath Prasad is my senior as a poet. His first collection of poems had appeared long before a poem of mine had been published in any magazine, and he had gained esteem as a rising young poet.'

On JP's poetry Prof. Sarbeshwar Das writes,

> During the first phase, Jagannath Prasad's poetry was greatly influenced by the Western, particularly the Eliotesque, sensibility. The theme of most poems is isolation, banishment, loneliness, desolation, emptiness, despair, uncertainty, pain, separation, and the awareness of death. But in the next phase, his poetry becomes

> outward looking; or, it may be said, there is a blend of the inward and outward visions. Different streams and forms of poetry blend in Jagannath's poetry. Being a painter, he creates striking visual images in his poetry which are highly original and spontaneous.

David McCutchion, a Scotsman who was Professor in the Department of Comparative Literature at Jadavpur University in the 1970s, produced a number of valuable studies which have been collected in the volume *Indian Writing in English: Critical Essays* (1968). In one of his essays he writes,

> How do we define Indian literature? Any literature is defined primarily in terms of the language in which it is written; and so the labels 'Odia literature' or 'Bengali literature' are self-explanatory. However, when we talk of 'English literature' in the past 200 or 150 years, we have to think of literature emanating from different countries, despite the use of a common language–for example, there is American literature, Australian literature, West Indian literature, etc. In this connection, it can be said, without much discussion, that any literary work which can be dignified with the label 'Indian' must have been translated into English and other Indian languages, regardless of the language in which it was originally written.

Prof. McCutchion thus emphasises writing in the 'indigenous' languages of India as well as in English.

Specific examples can be given here. It was only after Premchand's *Godan* was translated into English, about 50 years ago, that it was accepted as a pioneering work of Indian fiction. So also, Fakirmohan Senapati's *Chha Maan Atha Gunth* was acclaimed all over the country only after its English translation, published by the University of California, appeared in 2005. To put it plainly, a

J.P
1977

The Journey of Tales

JP's first book of poems, *Stabaka*, appeared in 1951; his first solo exhibition of paintings was held in 1961, but his first collection of short stories, *Bhabanath evam Anyamaney* (Bhabanath and others) was published only in 1982. The first story in this collection, 'Shabdabheda' (resolving the word), was written in 1980.

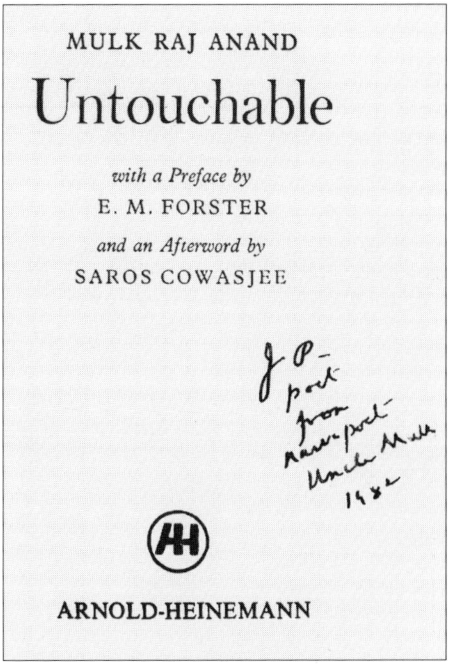

MULK RAJ ANAND

Untouchable

with a Preface by
E. M. FORSTER
and an Afterword by
SAROS COWASJEE

ARNOLD-HEINEMANN

JP's journey of creation began with poetry and painting; apparently, he was not interested in writing fiction then; we do not know why, nor do we need to. But his association with Mulk Raj Anand while in Delhi may have led to his trying his hand at short stories. As Anand wrote to JP in a letter in March 1980, 'If the incidental impact of my novel has made you turn time to time from poetry to prose, this is a welcome decision and I will claim credit for some part of your conversion. If only by saying that you were so bored with my book that you thought you could do better.'

FACING PAGE: *A doodle by Mulk Raj Anand*

ABOVE: *Autographed book presented by Mulk Raj Anand, 1982*

Poet Manu Dash's recollection deserves mention in this context.

> This happened in 1980 around Durga Puja. I was sitting at Kwality Press, founded by the late Jagdish Pani, which was the favourite meeting ground for writers in Bhubaneswar. Around noon the postman delivered some envelopes which my friend Asit Mohanty opened one by one. Several writers had sent stories for publication in the Puja number of the magazine *Samavesh*. Suddenly Asit danced in joy opening an envelope and went running to Jagdish Babu to inform him. Then he showed me the story entitled 'Shabda Athava Bhabnath Kahinki Pagal Hoi Gala' (Words or why Bhabnath turned mad) by Jagannath Prasad Das, his first story ever. Its striking caption, style, and subject matter made it different from all the other stories. It was, I recall, the most discussed story of the year.

Whatever were the circumstances under which JP started writing fiction, he is undoubtedly among the leading modern short story writers in Odia. Nearly all his stories can be found in the omnibus compilation *Katha Jatra* (the journey of tales). Chronologically, the individual volumes include *Bhabanath evam Anyamaney* (1982), *Dinacharya* (the daily routine) (1983), *Aamey Jeunmaney* (those of us) (1986), *Sakhyatkaar* (the interview) (1987), *Priya Bidushak* (dear jester) (1992), and *Shesha Parjyanta* (till the end) (1995). *Indradhanu* (rainbow), a collection of three of his stories, appeared in 2009. He was awarded the Sarala Purashkar for *Priya Bidushak*. So far, he has published 74 short stories.

With Nilamani Senapati, I.C.S., protagonist of the story Pucca Sahib, *1972*

In 2008, the National Book Trust asked me to edit a collection of Odia short stories written after Independence. It was difficult for me to decide which writers, and which of their stories, I should include. I sought the opinion of readers. Many of them wanted JP's story 'Loka Sanskruti' (folk culture) from the volume *Sakhyatkaar* to be selected. On reading the story, I felt it was truly representative and gave us an accurate picture of Odia and Indian society before and after Independence. Here is the story in brief.

> The writer returns to his ancestral village after nearly 25 years; this was where he grew up, but now he feels disconnected. However, some happy memories still linger and one of them is of the traditional Tiger Dance. The landscape has changed completely. He is driven to his family home, but that too has changed. The walls have been white-washed and a sign-board proclaims Tiger Dance Centre. Gopal, the writer's childhood friend and the son of a Tiger Dance guru, is its Director. Tiger Dance has acquired the status of a classical dance form and the Centre is visited by prominent scholars and critics of dance, foreign as well as Indian. One of the visitors, a white man, meets the writer, camera and tape-recorder in hand. The writer is reminded of the Tiger Dance of his childhood and the joyful ambience in which it was performed. Now the symptoms of commercialisation are evident. Feeling suffocated, he leaves the village.

Looking at the subject of this short story, one feels it could easily have been written as a novel. A tele-film based on the story was, however, produced.

JP's short stories have not received as much critical acclaim as his poetry or art criticism. Nevertheless, they do seem vast in scope and give us a useful insight into his life and time.

His story 'Priya Bidushak' deserves to be referred to here. It is about a writer and the characters he has created. It is his pen that has conjured up these characters, but they acquire a life of their own and assert their independence. As a result, the poor writer finds himself reduced to a jester.

This story tells us a great deal about the philosophy of life that informs JP's writing. He remains somewhat detached from his art, perhaps from life itself. Those who have known him closely believe that he accepts life as it comes and is undisturbed by circumstances. Critics have discovered this quality of detachment in his fiction as well. Critic Dasarathi Das writes,

> 'Jagannath Prasad Das is unattached to his characters, unbiased, and unemotional. As a painter, he is pitilessly aware of the environment. He depicts contemporary reality exactly as he sees it. This does not make his depiction photographic; rather, he makes it vibrant and credible through his imagination and experience of life. Life is entitled to be shown as it really is. Nowhere has Jagannath Babu attempted to glamorise or dramatise it. Artistic restraint is his speciality.'

In a review of 'Priya Bidushak' published in *The Deccan Herald* in 2004, Rashmi Vasudev writes, 'A sense of sadness pervades the stories, as in Conrad's "The Heart of Darkness". It makes the reader feel breathless and grow suspicious of the purpose of life, but one can find no cause for complaint. This is what the writer seems to want.'

These two critical opinions should not make us think that despair and disillusionment are the only elements in JP's stories, though they may predominate. Most of his characters are city-dwellers, middle-aged, and from the middle class, to whom gloom comes naturally. But occasionally the writer does return to the care-free childhood he has left behind, as in 'Loka Sanskruti'. His attachment to the joyful past peeps through the sadness. However, he remains more connected to today's reality, to what is happening. Another trait is the irony that keeps recurring. According to another critic, 'Irony is inherent to the structure of his stories, bringing to them a natural light-heartedness.'

JP's stories were written over a long period, between 1980 and 2009. He has not devoted so much time to any other form of art, apart from poetry.

The Odia short story is remarkably well-developed and evolved. In comparison, Odia drama and art criticism appear to be feeble. As a story teller, JP is skilled and is in tune with the younger generation. He seems contemporary to at least two generations of short story writers, from Kishori Charan Das, Shantanu Kumar Acharya, Krushna Prasad Mishra, Akhilmohan Pattanaik, and Manoj Das to Yashodhara Mishra, Debabrata Madanrai, and Gourahari Das. His success as a writer of short stories suggests greater discipline in his craft than in his art criticism or drama.

The period during which JP's short stories were written was one of transition for Odia society. The spread of education, specially among women, urbanisation, and industrialisation, had brought about transforming changes in life styles. The English language and western thought processes had impacted cultural life, and all this is reflected in JP's short stories. They are a clear reflection of our social attitudes. His style in these stories is refined, often straight forward. There is more concern with the depths of life and the delicate probing of experience than with the adornment of language. His view of life is generally internalised; events in the external world only lead to the unfolding of the inner consciousness. He raises more questions than he answers.

Meenakshi Mukherji writes about JP's fiction, 'The stories begin with clinical and detached descriptions, verging on reportage. But at some point, imperceptibly, the mood changes and we find ourselves in an unchartered territory, where shadows of unresolved mysteries darken the surface of quotidian life.'

In story after story, JP appears to be engaged in a dialogue with himself, and the conclusion that is reached is, life's mystery must remain a mystery.

Desha Kaala Paatra (1992) is the only novel that JP has written, but this one book has brought him more fame than many books written by some other writers, although reputations have been established on just the basis of a single novel, for example, Gopal Ballabh Das (*Bhima Bhuyian*), Baishnab Charan Das (*Maney Maney*), and Upendra Kishore Das (*Mala Janha*).

It is not easy to evaluate *Desha Kaala Paatra* using traditional yard sticks. As its theme is based on history, it could be called a historical novel; but it does not focus on a particular character or event. Its background is the social, political, and cultural history of 19th century Odisha, a confluence of the traditional and the emerging contemporary.

The book is a medley of characters and events, mostly familiar, but resurrected from the shadows of the past. The writer's intention was to hold the mirror to a particular epoch and in this he has succeeded.

Among the characters in the book we find Fakirmohan Senapati, Radhanath Ray, Gouri Shankar Ray, Pyari Mohan Acharya, Samanta Chandrashekhar, Madhusudan Das, Raja Ramchandra Deb, T.E. Ravenshaw, and John Beames, all of whom were leaders of Odisha in different fields. The decline of the Gajapati kings of Puri, the 'nine-digit famine', the agitation to preserve the Odia language, many such events are presented. The chronicle begins in 1859 and ends in 1907.

The publication of *Desha Kaala Paatra* had sparked off a great deal of discussion, even controversy, more than any other novel published in recent years. Whatever be the cause of the controversy, the publication of the book was acclaimed by all as a landmark. The prominent novelist Bibhuti Pattanaik wrote, '*Desha Kaala Paatra* is the best novel written in 1992'. The critic Sreenibas Mishra wrote, 'The authenticity of a historical novel and the refinement and stylistic elegance of a literary work make it an outstanding work.'

However, some critics did raise objections. According to them,

Cover of Hindi translation of Desha Kaala Paatra

- although parts of the book had been derived from various sources, no references had been made to the originals;

- in his depiction of iconic characters such as Fakirmohan Senapati and Radhanath Ray, the author had quite needlessly drawn attention to their weaknesses. Furthermore, third person singular forms of Odia verbs had been used to refer to them instead of the more respectful plural forms (e.g. Radhanath gala instead of Radhanath galey).

Those who criticised the factual content and the characters of the book were viewing it with reference to the genre of the historical novel. JP responded to these critics by saying,

- As the book had not been designed as an academic work addressed to scholars, there were no footnotes, bibliographical references, etc.
- Why should modern readers be reluctant to read about acts which Fakirmohan and Radhanath had not hesitated to confess a hundred years ago? (In the bowdlerised version of Fakirmohan's autobiography published by his son Mohini Mohan, certain portions relating to Fakirmohan's alcoholism, etc. had been excised, and editors who had restored them had done no wrong.)
- He had used verb forms such as 'gala' and '*kahila*' only when referring to Fakirmohan and Radhanath during their childhood or student days. When referring to them as mature adults, he had used the respectful forms.

How should persons of eminence be depicted in quasi-biographical fiction? One is reminded of the English writer Lytton Strachey in this context. In his *Eminent Victorians* published in 1918, he has produced brief biographical sketches of a number of eminent personages of the Victorian era. In his view, truly great people are great enough to be shown in their totality, 'warts and all'. Of course, many biographers are not in agreement with Strachey; they bring out only the best qualities of the persons they write about. This is what Surendra Mohanty has done in his two books, *Shatabdira Surya* and *Kula Bruddha*, based on the life of Madhusudan Das. JP obviously has a different view.

Prof. Jatindra Kumar Nayak, whose English translation of *Desha Kaala Paatra* appeared under the title *A Time Elsewhere*, wrote in a review,

> Constructing a counter discourse which gives a voice to the colonised is, however, one of the achievements of *Desha Kaala Paatra*. The narrative strategies the author employs in writing the social and cultural history of Orissa in the latter half of the 19th century account for much of our pleasure in reading the book. Unconfined by the conventions shaping the writing of scholarly history or fictionalized biography, the narrative shifts its focus constantly so that no single person or event dominates the centre-stage in the colonial drama. A picture of Orissa changing rapidly under alien rule is pieced together from fragments of biography. What gives coherence to this kaleidoscopic picture is the vision of decay followed by regeneration, which unifies the narrative.

The book gives us a sense of the high tide and ebb in Odisha's fortunes in the latter half of the 19th century. The three quotations which the author provides at the beginning of the book sum up his view of Odisha's history:

- 'This land is unconquerable; behind the aspirations of men lies the will of its protecting gods.' (Jaisingh, commander of Emperor Akbar's armies)

- 'Foreigners say that Odias are so thick-headed that they can never master any subject. But careful scrutiny will show that such a view is fallacious.' (*Utkal Dipika*, 2 September 1867)

- 'The dark night has ended.' (Radhanath Ray, 1892)

Desha Kaala Paatra is the saga of this unconquerable land. It is a story which cannot be forgotten.

JP in English Literature

Nearly all of JP's poetry and drama and many of his stories have been translated into English and his books on Pata paintings and palm-leaf manuscripts were written in that language. He himself has also translated into English two collections of Odia poems and one of Urdu. In other words, nearly his entire literary oeuvre is available in English, and this has helped him to win respect at the national level. His work has also been translated into Hindi and other Indian languages; but here, we shall look only at their English translations.

During the last six decades, several noteworthy efforts have been made to translate literary works from Odia to English. Utkal, Sambalpur, and Ravenshaw universities bestowed academic respectability on the enterprise of translation by making it part of the M.A. (English) curriculum. The Sahitya Akademi, National Book Trust, and Publications Division of Government of India, as well as prestigious publishers such as Oxford University Press, Macmillan, Penguin, and Orient Blackswan have brought out English translations of Odia works. In Bhubaneswar, institutions such as Satirtha, Rupantar, and Grassroots have been active in promoting translation. But most writers in Odia have had to depend on small local publishing houses for English translations of their work, usually at their own cost. So far, about 200 Odia books have been translated into English. Unfortunately, the translations

ABOVE: Dear Jester and Other Stories

and himself. Recently, Penguin published the English translation of his novel *Desha Kaala Paatra* by Jatindra Kumar Nayak. JP believes that translation of literary works by different translators, together with effective editing, helps to ensure quality.

As stated above, JP is translator of two collections of his own poems. The first, in which he collaborated with the French writer Catherine Clement was *Growing under an Indian Sky* (1991) and the second, in which Arlene Zide collaborated, was *Under a Silent Sun* (1992). The volume of Odia short stories in English translation edited by him, and the collection of poems translated into English entitled *Kavita* (1993) edited in collaboration with K. Satchidanandan, which appeared in 1983 and 1993 respectively, were also greatly appreciated. JP's English translation of Balaram Das' classic Odia poem *Lakshmi Purana* appeared in the periodical *Manushi* published from Delhi.

Here is what Paul St-Pierre has to say about JP as a translator,

> A few years passed before we were to meet again and collaborate on translations and editions of his own work—one book of short stories, *Dear Jester*, in collaboration with Rabi Swain, and two collections of poetry: *Lovelines* and *Dark Times*. These were occasions for me to see J.P. and work—responding immediately to queries and offering pertinent advice, checking the translation against the original and suggesting improvements, all with great attention to detail and a light and sure hand.

ABOVE:
With Ali Sardar Jafri and Mulk Raj Anand, 1980

LEFT:
With Anne Waldman and Jayanta Mahapatra, Sanchi, 1985

The corpus of his poetry in English translation was large enough for Prof. A.N. Dwivedi to include him in his anthology *Indian Poetry in English* (Arnold-Heinemann). He also edited a volume *Contemporary Indo-English Verse* in 1984 in which appears an article 'J.P. Das: An Appraisal' by K.G. Srivastava.

Critics have not, so far, paid adequate attention to his work as a translator while evaluating the entire body of his work.

Delhi Isn't Far

The address 305, Hauz Khas Apartments, New Delhi 110016 is known to many Odia writers and artists, who may have sent letters to it or received letters from it. This small flat in South Delhi is where JP has lived since his resignation from the IAS in 1984. I have not visited his house in Banpur in which JP lived during his childhood. But one can conceive of the similarity that exists between the house in Banpur, built sixty years ago, and the apartment in the metropolis of Delhi.

I have frequently had reason to visit the Hauz Khas flat. I had to travel to Delhi frequently between 2003 and 2007, while my second

FACING PAGE: *Sketch by Jatin Das, 2010*

LEFT: *With Odia writers celebrating Saraswati Samman to Manoj Das, 2001*

With Prof. G.K. Das, Ruth Vanita, and Yashodhara Mishra at a book launch in Delhi, 2001

FACING PAGE ABOVE: *Release of Complete Plays by Jaya Bachchan, 2013*

FACING PAGE BELOW: *With Paramita Satpathy, Keki Daruwalla, and K. Satchidanandan, at a book release, 2012*

son, Siddharth, was working for *The Times of India*, and it was then that I met JP at his Delhi home.

I found much that connected JP's personality and his writings to his home. All reflected the same transparency and neatness. His home was sparsely furnished; there were only a few paintings hanging on walls. There was no unsightly pile of books anywhere to suggest engrossment in work or study. He depends largely on the libraries at the Sahitya Akademi and India International Centre when he needs to consult any books. He possibly collects his facts on the Internet. When a book or periodical is no longer needed, it is given away to a friend or researcher; and yet, whenever he is asked a question, by letter or telephone, on any subject, literary or social, which he is unable to answer himself, he knows exactly where to look for the information. Rarely have I seen a more disciplined personality, or one more liberated.

Bijay Kumar Dash, former Public Relations Officer at the All India Institute of Medical Sciences, who lives in Delhi, once told me that there are about 6 lakh Odias living in Delhi and its surroundings.

Book
se by
SMT. JAYA
Saturday
tional Centr

Pretence

With Janaki Ballabh Patnaik and Narendra Kumar in a book launch in New Delhi, 1997

This may be only an estimate, but it is certainly not easy to feel the Odia presence in Delhi. Odias do not count for much in Delhi's political or commercial life, although the educated among Delhi's inhabitants are aware of their contribution to its administration and cultural activity. The bureaucrat, Lalit Mansingh, danseuses Sonal Mansingh and Kavita Dwivedi, and painter Jatin Das are well known. Quite a few Odia names come up in literary discourse: Jagannath Prasad Das, Ramakanta Rath, Sitakanta Mohapatra, Manoj Das, Pratibha Ray, and others. They write in Odia but their writings are available in English translation. Ramakanta Rath, Manoj Das, and JP have been awarded the prestigious Saraswati Samman while Sitakanta Mohapatra received the Jnanpith Purashkar. Ramakanta was President of the Sahitya Akademi and Sitakanta headed the National Book Trust. JP, however, is as wellknown as an art critic as he is as a litterateur.

JP is unique among Odia writers in that he has made Delhi his home and field of action. Civil service brought poets and writers here – Kishori Charan Das, Ramakanta, Sitakanta, Debdas Chhotrai, and

Haraprasad Das lived in Delhi for extended periods, but each one of them hurried back home after retirement, although story writer Chaudhuri Hemakanta Mishra had made Delhi his permanent home, until his untimely death in 2006. JP was the President of the Odia Samaj, established by Harekrushna Mahtab; he was also involved in the management of the Jagannath Temple in Hauz Khas and has contributed immensely to the social and cultural life of Odias in Delhi. His presence at meetings of the community is always of much importance.

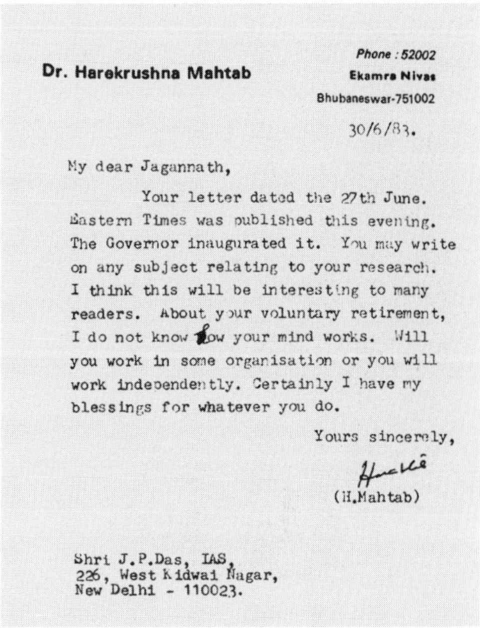

Dr. Harekrushna Mahtab

Phone : 52002
Ekamra Nivas
Bhubaneswar-751002

30/6/83.

My dear Jagannath,

Your letter dated the 27th June. Eastern Times was published this evening. The Governor inaugurated it. You may write on any subject relating to your research. I think this will be interesting to many readers. About your voluntary retirement, I do not know how your mind works. Will you work in some organisation or you will work independently. Certainly I have my blessings for whatever you do.

Yours sincerely,

(H.Mahtab)

Shri J.P.Das, IAS,
226, West Kidwai Nagar,
New Delhi - 110023.

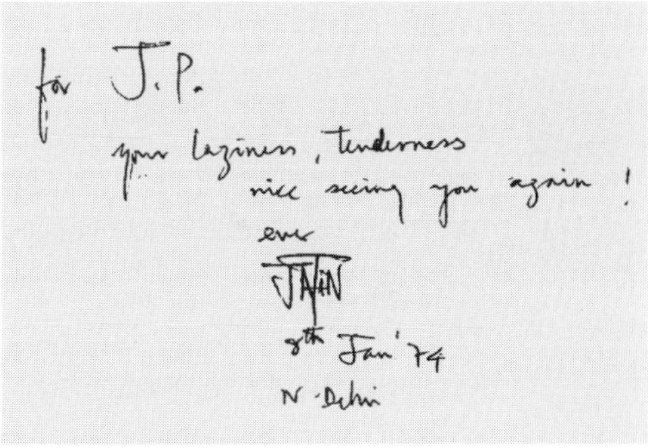

for J.P.
your laziness, tenderness
nice seeing you again!
ever
JATIN
8th Jan '74
N·Delhi

Till the end of the 1970s, Kolkata was the main centre of literary activity in Odia; but thereafter Delhi took its place. Poetess Kuntala Kumari Sabat chose Delhi for her sphere of literary activity as well as to practise medicine. This talented lady spent the last ten years of her life of 38 years (1900–1938) in Delhi. Kuntala Kumari was the first Odia writer to make Delhi her home and JP is an apt inheritor of the tradition she began.

Top: *Letter from Harekrushna Mahtab, 1983*

Above: *A note from Jatin Das, 1974*

It may be said that JP has been instrumental in bringing recognition and prestige to the Odia language and literature. Poets and artists from Odisha who visit Delhi consider their journeys incomplete unless they are able to meet JP. (It may be no coincidence that the Jagannath temple is also in Hauz Khas, where JP lives.) JP is friends with many poets, writers, artists, and social activists from

To Greener Pastures

TIME was when government service, especially in the prestigious IAS and IFS, was so coveted that many doing useful work in universities and the private sector grabbed every opportunity to get into the charmed circle. The traffic in the reverse direction which began some years ago is thus greatly to be welcomed though with one important reservation.

Some of the competent bureaucrats and diplomats have felt constrained to leave not because they felt that they had something more worthwhile to do in the groves of academe, research institutes or even the lucrative international institutions. They have quit because, in the inflamed political atmosphere since the mid-seventies, they have been needlessly pushed around.

Dr J. P. Das, the latest among the IAS officers to seek premature retirement, has done so, not because of any compulsion but out of choice. He belongs to the Orissa cadre and is at present his state's resident commissioner in New Delhi. His decision to retire 10 years ahead of schedule stems from a desire to devote his entire time to his literary and artistic pursuits.

During the last 25 years, while diligently doing a full-time job, Mr Das has written as many as 16 books, half of them in Oriya and the other half in English. His English works include "Puri Paintings", a research work on Pata paintings of Orissa.

A report in the Times *of India, 2 January 1984*

different parts of the country who live in Delhi. Among them are Mulk Raj Anand, Keki Daruwala, Meenakshi Mukherji, Jatin Das, Rajendra Yadav, Mannu Bhandari, and Madhu Kishwar. As member of the India International Centre, the India Habitat Centre, and the Press Club of India, he is in regular contact with many writers, artists, and civil servants. But what is most remarkable is that he gives as much importance to meeting young writers from different parts of Odisha as these VIPs from the Delhi circuit. To test the truth of this statement one merely has to write him a letter and see whether or not a reply is received.

I first visited JP's Delhi home about 30 years ago, when he was Odisha's Resident Commissioner in Delhi, residing in West Kidwai Nagar, an address few people might remember now. I was staying in Odisha Bhavan. Suddenly he called me up and invited me to dinner, and I accepted the invitation happily. Then he asked, 'How will you come?' answering the question himself, 'I'll go and fetch you'. It is easy to invite someone to your home in Delhi but difficult for the invitee to locate the correct destination and reach there safely, particularly for someone like me who does not know Delhi very well. Giving careful attention to every action, from preparing a cup of tea to correcting proofs, comes naturally to JP. He chose to pick me up and drop me back, rather than allow me to stray through the streets of Delhi. Could one have expected greater consideration from such a highly placed official?

In this book an attempt has been made to put together what many friends and admirers as well as critics of JP have said about

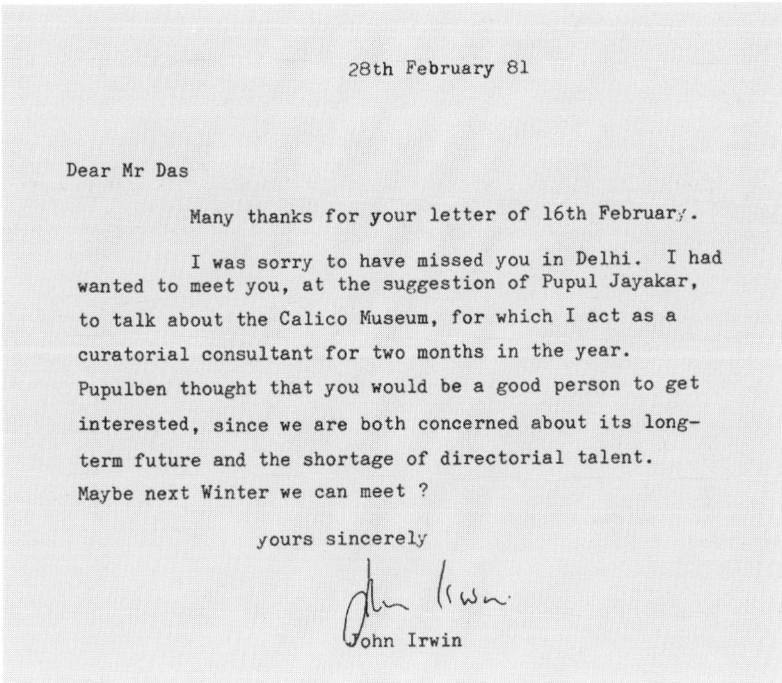

28th February 81

Dear Mr Das

Many thanks for your letter of 16th February.

I was sorry to have missed you in Delhi. I had wanted to meet you, at the suggestion of Pupul Jayakar, to talk about the Calico Museum, for which I act as a curatorial consultant for two months in the year. Pupulben thought that you would be a good person to get interested, since we are both concerned about its long-term future and the shortage of directorial talent. Maybe next Winter we can meet ?

yours sincerely

John Irwin

Letter from John Irwin, 1981

him. But no one has said anything about his mother Indu Devi. But here is what a friend of mine, Rankanath Hota, former Principal of Banpur College, has to say about the lady.

> The story goes back to 1947 when, at the age of nine, I was a student of Class 4 in Banpur High School and lived about 3 km away from the school. We had to trudge through muddy fields before we hit the road leading to the school, and the first house along the road was that of Shridhar Babu, who then taught at Christ College. His eldest son, Jagannath Prasad, lived with him at Cuttack. Sometimes it rained suddenly and we had to take shelter on the verandah of his house. In our eyes, it was a rich man's mansion. But Shridhar Babu's wife, Indu Debi, was like a mother to us and we all thought highly of her. She was plain-looking but very dignified and affectionate in her behaviour. No one ever heard her speak in a loud

In 1962

> voice. She would ask us questions like 'Which class are you in?' 'Why haven't you brought an umbrella today?' 'When did you have lunch?' and so on. Years have passed but we haven't forgotten her affectionate words, which took away our hunger and fatigue.

Doubtlessly, JP's personality–his friendliness and sympathy for those who suffer– has been shaped by his mother's goodness. Here is a letter from the mother to her son,

> Dear Jagan,
>
> Let me know how you are. Send me some photographs of the places you have been visiting. Do write at least once every week, so I can feel that I am looking at you.

> I am feeling depressed because you haven't written in a long time. I hope you are well. Our daughter's child has begun to turn over on her stomach and smile.
>
> Write soon.
> Your mother.

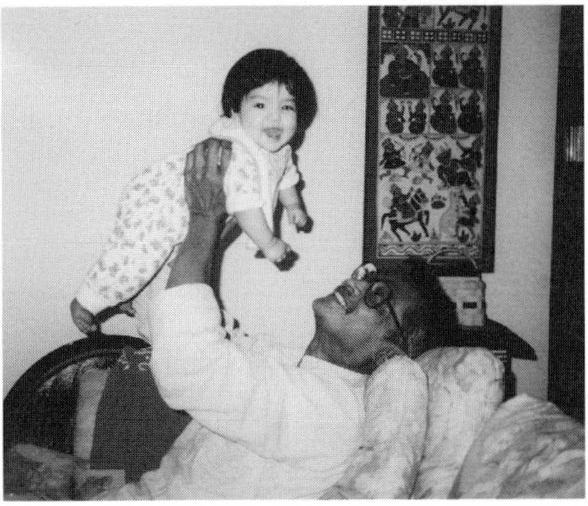

TOP: *With Mona, 1965*

ABOVE: *With Heena, 2000*

All mothers write such letters to their sons, yet each letter seems unmatched in its expression of feeling. This letter has been reproduced here as a mark of respect to the mother of a worthy son.

JP's 'Creative Journey' can have no conclusion, because he remains as active, as creative, and as dynamic as ever. The journey began in Banpur and proceeded to Cuttack, Allahabad, and Delhi. But even in Delhi, the journey continued. His only daughter, Mona, lives in America with her Japanese husband and their two daughters. The world outside sees JP as a pre-eminent personality, a leading poet, writer, and art critic. To his daughter, however, he is only a father, perhaps a perfect one. To his grandchildren he is an amusing grandfather. His inner persona comes through in this note from his daughter,

> My father was like a friend to me when I was growing up. He always treated me like an equal even when I was very young. He was a big favourite amongst all my friends;

With Mona and Mitra, 1987

till today they all remember how fun he was. He also had a great sense of humour and we used to laugh a lot together. He always encouraged me to try everything and to do and experience all kinds of things. He never put any pressure on me for anything and never imposed any expectations upon me. I always felt that no matter what I did, he would support me.

When I chose to marry outside our community, he never once made me feel that I had done something unacceptable. He has the amazing ability of accepting everyone just as they are. That is why he is very easy to be around with. He is a great grandfather to my children. He relates to them as someone of their age.

He never puts anything off till later. Anytime he has to do something, he does it immediately; so he is always current with everything. The other thing is how organised he is about everything. He even has all the report cards and letters from my childhood and also saved everything from my kids and gave them to me recently.

With Heena and Saachi, 2007

Another thing about him is how handy and skilled he is around the house. He can fix almost anything that needs fixing. He likes to be busy and never looks down on doing anything. Actually, I cannot think of anything he cannot do. He is extremely self-sufficient and can cook, stitch, iron, clean, and take very good care of himself. There are countless times I have left my children alone with him and he has taken care of them single-handedly and they always enjoy spending time with him.

All of his qualities make him a very unique person of his generation, times, circumstances, and culture. He has lived life mostly on his terms and not many people can claim that about their lives.

His granddaughter Saachi, aged 14 years, has this to say,

My grandpa, whom I call Booja because when I was a baby I mislearnt the word 'aja', is the most perfect grandfather in the world. Not only is he kind and caring, he is also very smart and funny. My sister and I always

With family, 2013

look forward all year long to see him every summer. Whenever we are with Booja, we have a lot of fun and spend every single free minute with him. He acts like he is our age when he is with us and does everything with us. He helps us with anything that needs to be done, makes food for us, plays with us, and we have a great time. At night, the three of us lie together and tell stories and jokes until late at night. He is so simple and fun that I forget he is such a famous writer. But he is a huge inspiration in my life and I hope to read all his books one day.

And here is Heena, aged 10,

> I love my Booja. He plays with me whenever I want and he helps me whenever I need help. He teaches me lots of stuff, some of the stuff is good but some of the stuff is how to be naughty. He hugs me and makes me feel better when I am sad. He does lots of fun things with me and takes me to lots of places. When we spend summer together, we do everything together. We eat, sleep, and play together and have lots of fun. He is the most fun grownup I know. He can fix anything and takes care of any problems we have. He is really smart.

Chronology of Events

1936–48	Birth and initial schooling at Banpur
1948	Shifted to Cuttack: Education in Mission School and Ravenshaw College
1951	Published collection of poems *Stabak*
1955–58	Allahabad University: Obtained Master's degree and started teaching
1958	Joined the Indian Administrative Service
1959	Started Serving Odisha Government
1960	Wrote plays *Made for Each Other* and *Miss X*
1963–66	Served as Collector, Kalahandi
1971	Holding of Painting Exhibition; Publication of *Pratham Purush*
1972	Wrote *Suryasta Purbaru*; staged in Bengla in Calcutta
1973	Moved to Delhi: Assignments with Government of India
1976	*Suryasta Purbar* staged in Hindi in Delhi
1979	Awarded Homi Bhabha Fellowship
1980	Publication of first short story
1981	Odisha Sahitya Akademi Award for *Je Jahara Nirjanata*
1982	Publication of *Puri Paintings: The Chitrakar and His Art*
1983	Appointed Consultant, Festival of India
1984	Vishuv Samman awarded by Prajatantra Prachar Samiti; Left IAS
1985	Founded Poetry Society (India); Appointed to the Board of Children's Film Society
1990	Central Sahitya Akademi Award for *Ahnika* (declined)
1992	Publication of *Desha Kaala Paatra* (*A Time Elsewhere*)
1998	Sarala Award for short story collection *Priya Vidushak*
2000	Awarded Nandikar, Kolkata Playwright Award
2006	Saraswati Samman for poetry collection *Parikrama*

Acknowledgements

Thanks are due to Vidyapuri, publisher, of the original book *Jagannath Prasad: Srujan Yatra* in Odia, for their kind permission to translate it to English; to Prof. Bikram K. Das, who translated the work; to Nityananda Misra and Gyan Asis Jena for helping out with selection of the images; and to Niyogi Books for publishing this book.

Index